CONTROLLING IT INVESTMENT

CONTROLLING IT INVESTMENT

STRATEGY AND MANAGEMENT

BEAT HOCHSTRASSER
CATHERINE GRIFFITHS

Consultants
Kobler Unit for the Management of
Information Technology
London

CHAPMAN & HALL

University and Professional Division

London · New York · Tokyo · Melbourne · Madras

Published by Chapman & Hall, 2–6 Boundary Row, London SE1 8HN

Chapman & Hall, 2–6 Boundary Row, London SE1 8HN, UK

Chapman & Hall, 29 West 35th Street, New York NY10001, USA

Chapman & Hall Japan, Thomson Publishing Japan, Hirakawacho Nemoto Building, 7F, 1-7-11 Hirakawa-cho, Chiyoda-ku, Tokyo 102, Japan

Chapman & Hall Australia, Thomas Nelson Australia, 102 Dodds Street, South Melbourne, Victoria 3205, Australia

Chapman & Hall India, R. Seshadri, 32 Second Main Road, CIT East, Madras 600 035, India

First edition 1991

© 1991 Beat Hochstrasser and Catherine Griffiths

Printed in Great Britain by
T.J. Press (Padstow) Ltd, Padstow, Cornwall

ISBN 0 412 43650 7

A catalogue record for this book is available from the British Library

Library of Congress Cataloging-in-Publication data
Hochstrasser, Beat.
    Controlling IT investment: strategy and management/Beat Hochstrasser and Catherine Griffiths. — 1st ed.
        p.   cm.
    Includes bibliographical references and index.
    ISBN 0–412–43650–7
    1. Information technology—Cost effectiveness. I. Griffiths, Catherine, BA, II. Title.
    HD30.2.H63   1991
    658.4′038—dc20   91–19798
                                                            CIP

Printed on permanent acid-free text paper, manufactured in accordance with the proposed ANSI/NISO Z 39.48–199X and ANSI Z 39.48–1984

CONTENTS

Contents

INTRODUCTION

Some companies are succeeding with Information Technology (IT) - most are not. Contrary to the expectations raised by a small handful of well-exposed case studies indicating how investments in IT have brought a company a strategic advantage, most managers find it difficult or impossible to replicate such success. All too often, companies report that large-scale IT deployment has simply resulted in replacing a set of old problems with a set of new problems, and that, overall, introducing IT can be a disappointment as unexpected difficulties are regularly encountered and as expected benefits are often not realised.

In the 1990s, IT is perceived primarily not as a technical issue but as a management issue. As the technology becomes more mature and reliable, the focus of management attention has shifted from controlling the technology to controlling the business, and the implications of the human and organisational impact of large-scale IT deployment. It is these that are now perceived to be the critical issues, issues that managers are only now beginning to understand:

- As a senior executive, are you finding it difficult to define the parameters of successful IT investments?

- Are you satisfied with the degree of integration between business goals, information flows and IT deployment in your company?

- Do you search for more reliable frameworks within which to plan further IT investments, for better methods of evaluating the risks against the benefits, and for practical guidelines on how to anticipate and deal with the broader organisational and human impact of large-scale IT deployment?

Some inspired individuals in a variety of organisations are addressing these issues and are currently developing a new generation of management tools, designed to enhance the business return on already installed technologies and to better control the return on further IT investments. Whereas these new tools do not necessarily guarantee success, it now becomes possible to treat IT investments not merely as 'an act of faith', but as a calculated risk, where the odds are increasingly known.

Controlling IT Investment collects the tactics, strategies and lessons learnt from best practice. The criteria that distinguish success from failure are identified, and practical guidelines are provided on how to manage and control not only the new technology, but also the broader human and organisational effects. The text, written for business managers rather than for IT professionals, is in the form of a book for senior executives which provides easily-accessible definitions, procedures, tables and check-lists on a wide range of business areas critically influenced by the introduction of IT. The book is based on an intensive three year programme of data collection and research at the Kobler Unit. Its principal aim is to fill the gap between the knowledge of what *should* be done to manage IT investments effectively, and what *is* done in practice.

Taking a broad operational definition of Information Technology as 'the set of all technological solutions to the problem of collecting, storing, manipulating and distributing information', Chapter 1 of the book analyses the growing concerns of British management towards traditional methods of managing and controlling the new technology. The following themes are discussed at length:

- What are realistic payback levels of IT investments?
- What are the most common cost elements that are often left unspecified when proposing, and evaluating, further IT

investments?

- What internal and external factors are distorting the projected return on the investments?

- How can traditional methods of investment evaluation be extended to cover sophisticated information systems?

- How can individual IT proposals be matched to specific evaluation techniques?

- What procedures are found to be most successful when allocating an IT budget and when distributing the responsibilities for IT investments?

- Are companies with an explicit IT strategy better off, and, if yes, are the benefits worth the considerable efforts of generating such a strategy?

- Does IT offer sustainable strategic business advantages, and, if not, are some companies gaining advantage by pooling infrastructure resources with competitors?

Looking at IT as a potentially effective tool to streamline the internal efficiency of a company, to enhance its external effectiveness and to develop entirely new markets, Chapter 2 presents a structured set of research data on the practical experience of over 50 managers in 34 companies in overcoming the barriers to improve their economics of scale and their economics of scope. The following questions are explored:

- How is the gradual deployment of IT best coordinated across a wide variety of business functions?

- Does IT need to be introduced according to an evolutionary path as many theoretical models want us to believe?

- If not, what are the alternatives?

- Are there competitive threats if a company is not effectively utilising the full potential of IT, and if so what are they?

Extensive research has revealed that successful companies are directing IT investments towards facilitating change. Chapter 3 of the book identifies and analyses the external forces that propagate change. The dynamic developments of an increasingly international business environment are investigated, and recent changes in customer demands, in employee expectations and in technological progress are analysed. The increasing strength of these forces strongly suggests that change is accelerating, and that further IT initiatives must be directed towards these new realities, or control over the investment will be lost.

Do you find, in your company, that large-scale deployment of IT is itself a force that drastically alters the internal dynamics of your organisation, and that, as a result, traditional reporting structures, rigid work allocations and ingrained cultural attitudes are often barriers to optimising your IT investment? Chapter 4 reveals how successful companies are tearing down these barriers by changing the overall shape of their organisation, by initiating a comprehensive programme of company-wide education, by raising both information and IT awareness, by introducing a new set of cultural values, and by encouraging risk taking and individual responsibility. Amalgamating the experiences of senior executives in these areas, the book discusses the relative success of various corporate initiatives to absorb change and to redefine the working relationship between a company and its employees.

Most managers are paying lip-service to the notion that IT is best introduced strategically across the organisation and that IT has to be strategically aligned to the direction of the business. Research shows that in current practice, well-defined theoretical models are difficult to apply within a business context, and that problems are encountered, which often lead to further dissatisfaction with IT investments.

- How do you translate the concepts of strategic IT deployment into actual business practice?

- What are the real strengths and weaknesses of alternative strategic methodologies?

- How can an IT strategy be aligned to a business strategy when the vast majority of companies report that their present market environment is too turbulent to allow the generation of an explicit business strategy covering a medium to long-term horizon?

- How can research data help to pinpoint the strategies that lead to success?

The book presents a methodology of how to establish independent criteria of organisational performance against which different IT investment strategies can be measured. Based on identified best practice, an explicit framework for strategic planning is given which recognises the disparities between theory and practice, and which enables management to coordinate and control strategic planning in a more dynamic and practical way. The starting point for the Kobler Unit Strategy Framework is not the generation of either a business or an IT strategy, but that of a corporate information strategy, based on a company's critical information flows. In Chapter 5, the detailed objectives of such an information strategy are spelt out, its parameters clearly defined and its individual elements extensively discussed. Practical guidelines for applying the framework are given by combining traditional top-down and bottom-up planning approaches into a new participatory approach designed to introduce a constructive dialogue between top management, IT management and the user community.

Chapter 6 consolidates insights gained and deals directly with the definition, the planning, the implementation and the management of a corporate IT strategy. A well-defined IT strategy framework is given and the variety of issues that the strategy must address are amalgamated and discussed. Planning is supported by presenting the model of a migration path leading from current realities to an aspired future scenario and by the introduction of multiple dimension priority-setting for individual projects. Management issues of implementation are highlighted by analysing the main reasons for failure, and good practice of successful management of the strategy over time is supported by incorporating lessons learnt on how to implement managerial control over IT investments.

ACKNOWLEDGEMENTS

We are sincerely grateful to the many individuals, both in industry and in academic research, who have participated in the current investigations. In particular, the authors wish to thank Professor Igor Aleksander, Professor Bruce McA. Sayers, Paul Strassmann, and Leslie Willcocks.

CHAPTER 1

DIAGNOSING GROWING CONCERNS

As IT investments continue to take a large and growing proportion of the annual budget, executives and senior managers are increasingly concerned about the validity of traditional approaches taken to identifying effective IT investments, to evaluating IT initiatives, and to subsequently managing IT investment.

The Kobler Unit has identified a situation where for most companies management concerns have ousted technical concerns. Managers continue to experience situations where the application of IT produces results of dubious benefit and often quite unrelated to current business aims. Companies are struggling to harmonise their existing IT involvement with business goals to be achieved, while at the same time being pressurised by demands from users and from their own IT departments to increase spending further, as current installations are declared to be incomplete or incompatible.

A number of recent IT surveys have shown that investments in IT often fail to deliver acceptable returns. It is reported that:

- in some quarters the commitment of senior management to IT is minimal, possibly reducing (PA Consulting Group, 1989)
- IT seldom leads to sustainable competitive advantage beyond market norms (Booz, Allen & Hamilton, 1989)

- IT is not linked to overall productivity increases (OECD, 1988)

- IT overhead costs are consistently larger than anticipated (A.T. Kearney, 1987)

- project deadlines are seldom met (Price Waterhouse, 1988/89)

- despite the introduction of marketing information systems, the biggest identified disappointment to managers interviewed was that sales have not increased to overall expectations (OASiS, 1989)

- only a very few organisations succeed in educating staff to best use IT already installed (BIM, 1988)

- an average of 70% of information systems installed per company are not run effectively (Trade and Industry Committee, 1988)

- 70% of companies (*Business Week*, 1989) state that MIS lead to confusion by generating information overload

- investment decisions are largely 'an act of faith' as 75% of companies lack any effective evaluation procedures for new IT initiatives (Peat Marwick, 1989)

- integrating IT with corporate plans is 'the major IT problem' facing management today (Price Waterhouse, 1989/90)

- 70% of users declare that their systems were not returning their company's investment (Romtech, 1989)

- only 15% of companies following an IT strategy regard their strategy as 'highly successful' (Sheffield/A/Anderson, 1988)

- only 31% of companies report that the introduction of IT has been 'very successful' (Amdahl Research Report, 1988).

The current study has investigated those concerns which can best be captured by asking the following questions, which are very much on the minds of senior managers:

- Is IT value for money? If the ROC on IT investments turns out to be consistently below expectations, as many studies claim, what other reasons are there for continuing IT investments at the present levels?

- How can IT initiatives be evaluated? As it is often not possible to spell out bottom line benefits in well-defined financial terms, how is it best decided what to plan and implement?

- How much is to be allocated for IT? Is there a figure or a ratio that a company should aim for when allocating an IT budget? Or is a fixed annual IT budget itself a constraint on the flexibility needed to react to changing needs?

- Who is to take responsibility for IT investments? How can a company best combine the knowledge of business managers and IT professionals into a joint effort to manage the investment?

- Is there a need for an explicit IT strategy? Is IT important enough to warrant the effort? What are the disadvantages, as experienced by companies who are proceeding without a corporate plan?

- Does IT offer strategic advantages? Is it a strategic and competitive *dis*advantage not to have adequate IT support?

1.1   IS IT VALUE FOR MONEY?

Company managers today are increasingly concerned that the much-heralded payback from their IT investments may not be forthcoming. The current research has found that while 68% of companies interviewed treat IT expenditures as a normal capital investment which has to show a definite return, there is no longer the automatic assumption that IT is good value for money. In fact, there is widespread disagreement among managers from different companies and even among managers within the same company, about the true value of large-scale IT investments.

This wide dispersion of opinion is shown in the following graph:

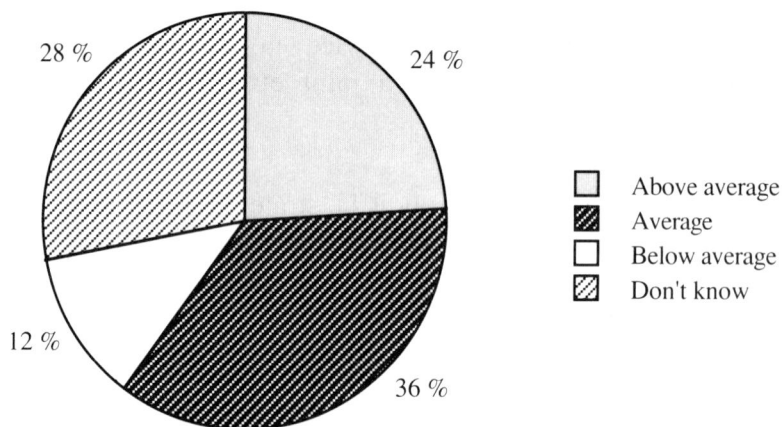

**Figure 1.1 How does the return on capital of your IT
investment compare to other investments?**

- Management's reluctance to assume that IT pays off is highlighted by the fact that more than a quarter, 28%, of managers interviewed acknowledge that they are not using strict procedures for calculating how the return on capital of their IT investment compares to the ROC of other investments. Given that the amount of money spent on IT is substantial to say the least, this is indeed a surprising result showing the widespread need to introduce acceptable methods and standards for the evaluation of IT investments.

- The study further shows that one in eight, 12%, of companies are clearly disillusioned with the payback they obtain, and declare the ROC of IT to be below average when compared to other investments. Despite this, however, further discussion revealed that most companies within this sample are not considering pulling out of IT but are planning to further increase their IT investment over the next three years.

- Managers in the largest group, comprising 36%, rate the ROC of their IT investments to be on a par with other investments. However, it was noted that these ratings are often based on subjective opinions and that not all managers within the same company agree.

- Only 24% of companies are positive that their IT investment shows a ROC that is above average when compared to other investments. Of these, a high proportion can point to company-wide standards of strict evaluation procedures subscribed to by all managers in the firm.

Given the general lack of confidence in the value of IT, it became imperative to establish the reasons why companies have been investing and are continuing to invest in IT.

The following results were obtained:

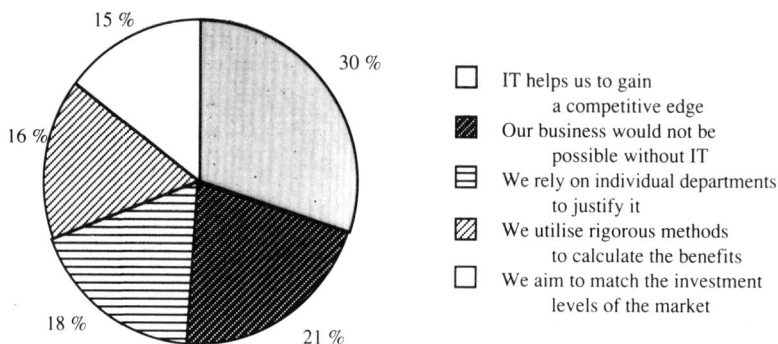

Figure 1.2 What is the main reason for your
investment in IT?

- When companies are asked why they invest in IT, it transpires that only 16% of managers rely on rigorous methods to calculate the benefits. As management procedures for evaluating the return on other investments are usually very strict, in fact as the quality of such procedures is often correlated directly with long-term business survival, this is a most surprising result. It suggests either that there is something inherently different in the approach used to evaluate IT investments, or that the majority of managers simply do not have adequate tools at their disposal to evaluate the benefits of IT.

- An almost equal number of companies, 15%, are satisfied with achieving a close approximation to the norm of their respective market sector by aiming to match the investment levels of competitors. The rationale behind this approach is based on the belief that in uncertain circumstances, safety can be found by joining the majority.

- A slightly larger proportion, 18%, shift the responsibility to individual departments to justify the investment. This study has found that when individual departments are burdened with justifying their IT installations to senior management, the most widely used method for doing so is to rely upon a system of periodic reporting. It was noted, however, that the emphasis in these reports is generally more on the assessment of technical performance, rather than on whether the system actually delivers a valuable service directed to meeting corporate business objectives.

- The second largest group, 21%, state that IT investments are justified not by evaluating benefits but simply by the fact that the company could not exist without its current IT involvement. It is then explained that IT systems are the only way to cope with today's volume and complexity of data. The dependency of companies on IT is further illustrated in a recent report published by the PA Consulting Group for the Government, entitled *Top Management Information Systems in Whitehall*, which on the one hand acknowledged the Government's main priority to achieve value for money in the public sector - especially with regard to IT expenditure - and on the other hand stipulates that government departments simply could not be managed in the first place without large-scale utilisation of IT.

- The most popular justification for investing in IT, mentioned by 30% of managers, is that IT helps companies to gain a competitive advantage. Innovative use of IT has enabled many companies to offer a better customer service and to raise the quality of the products sold. Furthermore, it is pointed out that new business functions, such as global trading, directly depend on the successful use of the new technology. However, such advantages are often short lived, as competitors eventually acquire the facilities to exploit the new technology in a similar manner.

Summarising the response received, it has become evident that only very few companies consistently state that IT is indeed value for money. IT investments are not generally regarded as a high payback investment. In fact, most companies do not realise their projected return on capital. The current study has also shown that most companies find it difficult to provide solid reasons for why they are continuing to invest in IT. However, additional findings, discussed later on, indicate that companies are poised to spend even more money on IT over the next few years than ever before.

It must be concluded that once a company starts to invest in IT, demands to further increase the investment will automatically follow. In this sense, investing in IT has become like driving down a one-way street. Once the course has been set, there is no turning back. The company has lost control of the direction and is forced to continue down the same road, propelled by the momentum of previous IT investments.

1.2   HOW CAN IT INITIATIVES BE EVALUATED?

The current research examined the quality of different evaluation procedures by comparing the originally projected set of expected benefits of proposed IT initiatives with subsequent studies showing the set of net benefits actually achieved.   Three observations can immediately be made. Firstly, before a company can evaluate the payback of its IT investments, a solid method has to be set in place to assess the true costs involved, including technological costs, human costs, and organisational costs (see Appendix C). Case studies suggest that human and organisational costs might well be four times as high as hardware/software costs. Secondly, to be relevant, evaluation procedures have to assess both primary objectives of proposed systems, and the potential positive and negative second order effects resulting from subsequent organisational change. Thirdly, evaluation procedures exclusively based on standard accounting methods simply do not work. In the majority of cases, evaluation cannot be restricted to the measurement of immediately obvious financial cause and effect relationships by proving that a particular benefit is directly and solely caused by a particular system.

To evaluate the primary objectives of IT initiatives, the current study has found that no single generic procedure exists for measuring the variety of functions and benefits that have been made possible or are supported by the application of IT. Doctrines which claim that a single approach suffices are increasingly being recognised as inadequate and restrictive, in evaluating most of today's sophisticated IT installations. It is often not possible simply to regard IT evaluation as being based exclusively on spelling out bottom line benefits in well defined financial terms. The main drawback from such a practice is that whenever it is difficult to pinpoint the exact correspondence between a particular benefit and a particular IT installation, the inclination is to quantify what is easy to measure rather than what is important. Thus, the resulting quantification might be accurate but irrelevant. Examples of major costs difficult to assess at the pre-evaluation stage include indirect staff and management costs, loss of productivity during installation times, loss of time and energy from devising and implementing IT-related policies, and loss of continuity as wider organisational changes become imminent. Similarly, benefits which are impossible to quantify in the short term include the installation of corporate infrastructure core systems that offer individual divisions the opportunity to subsequently develop their own applications, and systems installed for the purpose of maintaining or improving the competitive position of a company.

If it is acknowledged that evaluation procedures have to take account of the potential of IT for opening up pathways to become more effective in the medium to long term, the primary objectives of IT initiatives can be evaluated by matching specific evaluation techniques to specific application areas:

- IT systems that are introduced to increase the accuracy of information, to enable management to take on additional tasks, to speed up the business cycle or to automate cumbersome, laborious manual activities related to information processing, eg. Optical Character Recognition systems to automate the input of written material, are best evaluated by the well understood techniques of cost benefit analysis, like Stages Survey (Index Group, 1987) and Direct Labour Cost Substitution (A.T.Kearney, 1987). These methods have grown from industrial engineering approaches, and are based on cost elimination and on increased data volume. For instance, the benefits of an automated payroll system can be strictly quantified in terms of staffing levels and better money management. Similarly, the upgrading of an existing information system by a new system can be quantified either by the new system being cheaper to run while offering the same functionality, or by the new system costing the same but offering an increased functionality.

- IT systems introduced to increase staff productivity, to utilise resources better, or to offer better information sharing within a company can be evaluated by Value Chain Analysis (Porter, 1980), Value Linking and Value Acceleration. These techniques serve to evaluate the potential of IT deployment to transform the value chain to a firm's advantage. They are extensions of traditional value added methodologies, and assess the benefits of a particular system both by the improved quality the new service offers to other departments, and by the actual utilization of the new facilities. Improved services can be gained through the provision of better information or through reduced timescales. To establish how services can be improved, value added techniques presuppose that managers, when well prepared, can be held accountable for stating their exact information needs. The firm then fulfills these needs with as little investment as possible. The benefits of a corporate-wide network, for example, are then evaluated by assessing the facilities available, and by measuring the amount of information that is actually requested over the system by individual managers. This model also applies to non-profit making organisations, as it analyses the mechanics rather than the economics of organisations.

- IT systems introduced to improve product quality or to offer better services to customers can be evaluated by methods derived from the Customer Resource Life Cycle (Ives & Learmonth, 1987). The rationale behind this approach is based on the philosophy that customers are the life-blood of a company, and as such demand full attention and optimal service. It is then proposed that customers perceive a company's products differently over time and that this perceptual change is locked into a life-cycle of eleven stages. The method can be used to evaluate the degree to which the system to be installed will fulfill critical needs of customers throughout this life-cycle. For example, a help desk facility can be justified by the critical need that customers expect such a service (if indeed true) when they first start dealing with a company. Evaluating a possible installation of extensive communication links with customers can be justified by the need as perceived by customers, that such installations are indeed critical for securing their continued loyalty at more mature stages of their life-cycle, and by the opportunity of 'locking in' customers, by creating switching costs.

- IT systems introduced in order to strategically exploit the potential of the new technology to do things that were not possible before, can be justified by risk evaluation techniques. These techniques take into account that the investment is insecure, but promises a potentially high payoff that is ultimately justified by possible drastic cost cutting, or by a greatly increased market share. The nature of risk taking is such that a bottom line quantification based on a cost-benefit analysis is not possible beforehand, and that informed judgements have to be made. These judgements can only be made by someone understanding the dynamics of the market and not, for example, by an internal IT evaluation team. The investment therefore has to be justified by those actually taking the risk.

To evaluate second-order effects of IT initiatives, the social and political implications of large scale IT deployment have to be taken into account. Introducing IT into a company always brings about wide ranging changes in the way a company is structured and in the way people work. These effects can result in radical shifts in job descriptions, salary structures, the role of middle management, and in traditional divisions between functions. Introducing IT often forces a company to completely redesign the shape of its organisation. It was also noted that some organisations have been vulnerable to hijacking by small but strong interest groups seeking power and status. Evaluations of IT initiatives have to take these potential effects into account by judging a company's ability to control the internal dynamics of organisational change. In practice, such evaluations can be based on instituting regular discussions between all groups affected by the introduction of IT. The backdrop to these meetings has to be a climate where open debate is possible, and where the discussion is not couched in the technical terms of the system provider, but in the language of the information user.

Often the payback from an IT system depends on successfully mediating between groups of people who have different interests, particularly when changes are proposed in the distribution of corporate power relating to the control of vital information. An example is the introduction of a sophisticated distributed customer database containing both 'hard' data like purchasing history, and 'soft' data like purchasing preferences, plans, rumours, or other inside information. Such a database, accessible to all, might be resisted by some managers who currently control access to vital customer data, on the grounds that to release control on that data might weaken their own political position within the company.

The level of commitment of all users to a particular IT system has to be established. Running or introducing an expensive IT installation which, according to technical specification, could save the company money, or could offer potential business benefits, can be very cost ineffective if the system is not used to its full potential by all parties concerned. A low level of commitment is particularly conceivable if large scale retraining, redundancies or redeployment of staff are involved. For instance, if certain groups resist change and misuse facilities, introducing an office automation system can disrupt current business routines and be harmful rather than beneficial to the flow of internal communication .

An eclectic approach to IT evaluation needs to be taken which matches different types of IT applications and different types of projected organisational change to specific evaluation techniques. Due to the dynamic factors inherent in IT investments, evaluation must be regarded as a continuous process which needs to be kept under review at regular intervals. It cannot be tenable to justify a policy proclaiming a single one-off evaluation procedure. Without regular re-evaluation, potential further benefits can be missed on several counts: the technology itself may develop to a stage where cheaper technical solutions become viable, users may outgrow the current system, or the demands of the market environment in which a company operates may change so that older systems no longer address current needs.

The lack of relevant and regular evaluation procedures leads to loss of control of IT investments. Without relevant evaluation procedures, the introduction of IT is based on an act of faith - without repeating these procedures at regular intervals, benefits once achieved may no longer be realised.

Evaluation is often conceived of as a purely post-implementation process of retrospective assessment which provides only historic insight. The current study has found that where indicators of effective performance have been developed and are used for regular monitoring, the process of evaluation is easily extendible to help with the selection of new projects, by assessing IT initiatives at the pre-implementation stage, before the actual investment is made. As such, the development of a comprehensive evaluation programme is not an overhead, but an investment in a valuable tool for supporting a company's strategic IT deployment.

1.3   HOW MUCH IS TO BE ALLOCATED FOR IT?

Every financial year, at budget allocation time, senior managers ask themselves whether the newly proposed funding levels for IT investments are reasonable and what criteria should be employed to decide future investments. Doubts arise when considering whether it is indeed constructive to allocate a fixed annual budget as fiscal considerations demand. Further uncertainties arise when it is realised that every centrally allocated pound for IT is matched by a large percentage in spending by individual departments. The decision is difficult, because, on the one hand, processing power can be acquired more cheaply every year, and on the other hand, the demands to spend more constantly increase.

The Kobler Unit is often asked to provide a company with a figure or a ratio that should be aimed at when allocating an IT budget. However, previous research by the Unit questions whether an ideal level of IT spending really exists, and whether the attempt to identify such a level is helpful when deciding which IT projects are to be approved.

In searching for an ideal level of IT spending, a frequently used criterion is to compare a company's investment levels with the norm of their respective market sectors. According to a survey of 750 companies, published by Price Waterhouse in their Annual IT Review, the average IT budget as a percentage of turnover is close to 1%.

An additional criterion frequently employed to find an ideal level of IT spending is to base new investment levels on the commitments of previous years. The current study collected figures indicating that while in the years 1986 and 1987 IT budgets generally decreased by 5 - 15%, new levels of spending have increased again by roughly the same factor. Similar figures have been obtained elsewhere. A recent survey by Peat Marwick McLintock of 103 of the top UK companies and 51 public sector organisations, showed that the average increase in IT budgets in the coming year is between 14% and 25%. This trend has further been substantiated by Price Waterhouse's Annual IT Review, indicating that a general increase of about 11% is expected.

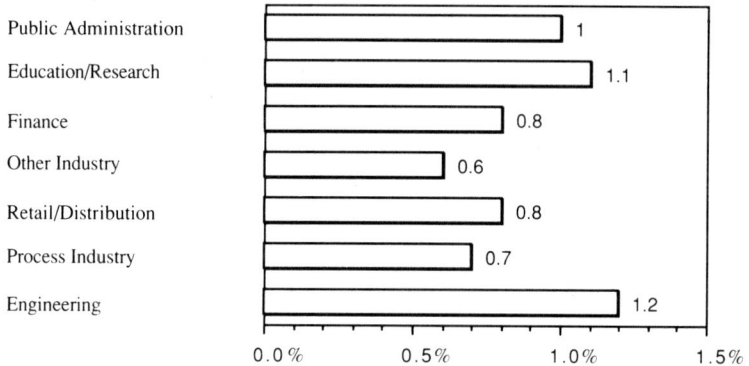

Source : Price Waterhouse, 1989

Figure 1.3 IT budgets as a percentage of turnover in industry sectors in 1988.

Both these criteria, to conform to market norms or to previous commitments, are particularly favoured by members of a board who are not entirely confident about understanding the implications of the new technology and who hope to gain a sense of security by being well in tune with the market. This approach is also favoured by many IT managers, partly for reasons of keeping a tag on the level of competitors' investments, and partly for reasons of gaining political bargaining power when proposing new IT installations.

While it is conceded that awareness of competitor spending and market norms can be very valuable, particularly when a company decides to invest on disparate levels, Kobler Unit results have shown that these are not critical factors when evaluating the actual return on the investment. Indeed, the hypothesis that there exists an ideal level of IT spending to which all should adhere, has been discredited by the current study, as it can be shown that different companies direct their IT towards different tasks, control and manage their investment in different ways, and subsequently achieve a different return on their initial outlay.

The notion that investment levels ought to be based on a company's specific commitments from previous years is often accompanied by the expectation that as a company expands over time, its IT investment level should increase as well. The rationale behind this idea is that IT must grow in relation to turnover and profit. However, the hypothesis that a larger level of IT investment brings more benefits has not been substantiated by the research of the Unit. Indeed, it has been shown that no statistical correlation exists between the overall amount spent on IT and actual business success (Kobler Unit, 1988).

Whatever level of investment is chosen, a strict allocation of a fixed annual IT budget is itself problematic. In the past, it has been common practice to set aside a specific sum for IT, and then to let individual divisions tender for allocations through presentations of well argued business cases. However, more recently, many companies feel that this practice should be changed, as it often does not make sense to try to contain sophisticated IT projects within single divisions. Many current projects, especially in the areas of communication, data exchange, and distributed corporate databases, are by their nature cross-divisional efforts and have to be implemented and managed by a team with a corporate and not a divisional perspective.

Other companies point out that the allocation of a fixed annual IT budget prior to the identification of the actual application areas and the costs of the technology, make it impossible to evaluate the return on the investment at budget allocation time. In a climate where open-ended faith in the benefits of technology has been replaced by the demand for strict evaluation procedures, such a practice has become increasingly unacceptable.

At the other end of the spectrum, end users argue that as changes in the market situation and in IT are accelerating, fixed annual budgets are simply too restrictive and result in lost business opportunities.

The present study therefore suggests that comparative studies of expenditure between one company and another are of less interest than whether the expenditure is regarded as an investment generating a positive return, is focused on long-term stability rather than on short-term gains, and is well balanced between efficiency and effectiveness gains. The absolute level of expenditure on IT is then perceived as a function of identified business needs, as the ability to analyse these needs and as the maturity of the new technology to deliver practical and cost effective support to fulfill these needs. While the allocation of absolute funding levels for IT is neither helpful nor desirable, the present study has shown that the true costs of IT are often not appreciated by management. Indeed, it transpires that cost containment for IT is now becoming a key issue for management to address. The old question of 'how much do we allocate for IT?' is therefore superseded by the new challenge, 'how do we control IT costs?'

To control IT costs, management has to strengthen its grip on the policies currently in place for authorising user and departmental expenditure on IT. Furthermore, management has to be aware of the areas where it is most likely for additional costs to arise. Lastly, management has to control demands by the IT department for further investments aimed at upgrading existing systems, rather than at delivering tangible business benefits.

The majority of companies have policies in place which prescribe different approval procedures for large-scale and small-scale IT investments. The dividing line is often an amount around ten thousand pounds. While large-scale IT investments then have to be endorsed centrally, small-scale investments can be authorised locally under a number of different procedures. This makes it very difficult to pool all the costs involved and to get a figure for a company's overall IT investment. What is not known about, cannot be controlled. The current set of case studies indicate that 30 - 50% of the total IT spending in companies is authorised outside the official IT budget. These observations are similar to figures collected elsewhere. For example, according to the Price Waterhouse Review 1987/88, small companies spend 38% on IT outside the IT budget, while large organisations spend 32% on IT outside the officially allocated budget. Unless a company is aware of its true expenditure on IT, it will not be in a position to control future investment levels.

It is a well known fact that IT projects often cost more than was originally planned. The current study has found that the largest uncontrolled IT costs stem from:

- small but regular hardware costs like PCs, drives, printers, cables or disks
- environmental costs like rewiring, air conditioning, new furniture or office redesign
- loss of business if the system is malfunctioning
- rising salaries of IT support staff
- access fees to external systems
- time spent installing new systems
- time spent configuring or reconfiguring software

- time spent learning new applications
- time spent evaluating systems at regular intervals
- consultancy and training fees.

A recurring theme during this study is the observation that introducing IT brings about change. Often that change has a momentum of its own. This is particularly true when the demands for further investments are analysed. The new technology can be very seductive in the sense that investments in additional gadgets or in the newest power applications are hard to resist - especially when such demands are formulated in the language of the technology, a language that many senior managers are hard pressed to understand. This danger has to be recognised and the temptation to automatically endorse such demands has to be resisted. A policy has to be put into place to the effect that *all* investment proposals have to be evaluated in terms of fulfilling actual business needs.

1.4 WHO IS TO TAKE RESPONSIBILITY FOR IT INVESTMENTS?

Traditionally, the responsibility for all investments, including investments in IT, has remained firmly with the Finance Director. This tradition is being questioned by a number of companies in the present study who are increasingly concerned that as their IT involvement has grown in size and begun to affect a wider range of business functions, it has become exceedingly difficult for any single person to fully appreciate the complexity of issues involved. Companies point out that large-scale introduction of IT has generated a new and powerful information infrastructure, and that the dangers to the core business if the technology is mismanaged have risen proportionally with every pound invested and with every system installed.

Responsibility for IT investments cannot be divorced from organisational and human issues, and entails much more than evaluating the technical feasibility of individual investment proposals:

- Projects cannot be allocated in isolation, but often have to be coordinated with one another.

- An overall plan has to be put into place which prioritises different implementations according to the importance of the business objectives to be achieved.

- Resources have to be allocated and monitored across different projects and departments.

- Systems have to be re-evaluated at regular intervals, as the specifications of any complex installation are never static but change as market situations develop and new business opportunities become apparent.

- A company-wide policy has to be put into place to protect electronic data against loss.

- Emergency plans to conduct business have to be made in case computer systems break down.

- Data security arrangements have to be implemented.

- The continuous support and training of staff working with computers has to be organised and assured.

- A central function has to be implemented and managed which monitors all IT-related issues across all departments in order to ensure that the company as a whole learns optimally from its IT experience.

- Technological 'windows of opportunity' have to be monitored continuously.

In many large companies, the responsibility for IT investments, after the original decision to invest and to implement has been taken, is often left either to the IT department or to individual users. The problem is that while users themselves often want to deal with supporting small and individual desk-top applications, the responsibility for maintaining, supporting and updating the basic infrastructure system common to many users across several divisions needs to be centralised. Equally, a corporate adherence to a common set of standards and methods is desirable.

As companies realise that effective systems are not just implemented, but have to be developed over time, user involvement becomes paramount. Regular feedback by end users on the performance of current systems and on possible extensions of a system's functionality can be essential to sustain a positive payback on the investment. This is only possible if both users and IT professionals engage in a mutual effort. The reality is, however, that most companies are still struggling to establish effective ways to harness the valuable contributions users can make towards developing new systems.

One of the major problems facing management today is how to generate a corporate atmosphere which facilitates the sharing of business and of IT knowledge. Many companies are caught in a cycle where IT professionals state that if they knew the business better they could say how IT might help, and where business managers maintain that if they knew what was technically possible, they would be able to tell if IT could assist them. The problem is that both business managers and IT professionals think in highly developed concepts, and find it hard to communicate to outsiders in simple terms. Success with the introduction of IT can only be achieved if the investment is managed dynamically beyond the actual implementation process, and regular attention is given to both the technical and human issues involved. The introduction of IT is not an event but the beginning of a continuous process of assessment, evaluation, and development, which has to be maintained and controlled. This necessitates a close working relationship between decision makers, users and IT providers.

When companies were asked what they considered to be the main constraints to optimising their IT involvement, it transpired that three out of four suffer from communication gaps between senior managers and IT professionals:

- 38% of companies state that a poor understanding of the potential of IT by senior management is a constraint
- 35% of companies consider themselves constrained by a poor understanding of business plans by IT professionals.

If senior managers with little knowledge of IT take charge of IT, the resulting systems tend to be expensive, patchy and only used to a fraction of their full potential. Incompatibility problems between different in-house installations often arise and the same data has to be input repeatedly for different functions, leading to duplication and error. Eventually, further technology has to be brought in, in the attempt to correct original mistakes.

If IT managers with little knowledge of business goals are left in charge of IT, the emphasis in planning IT projects tends to be placed on the technological aspects of IT, such as the accuracy and speed of output, rather than on the appropriateness of business functions supported. Often, this leads to information overload where management cannot easily access salient information. In a technologically-based approach to IT investments, systems tend to be awkward to use and therefore result in frustration and in higher training costs. As many users have to learn repeatedly, technological feasibility does not necessarily imply practical usability. For instance, in one company interviewed, the IT department had recommended the installation of a complex Office Automation system. It was argued that current business functions like receiving orders, referring to case histories, booking appointments, and scheduling resources, could all be transferred to the computer. After 12 months all these functions were indeed computerised. However, given the time and the resources available, it proved impossible to integrate the different programs into a coherent whole, and users had to step through complicated log-in and log-out procedures to move from one application to the other. As a result, the system proved too difficult and time consuming to operate, and rapidly became very unpopular. In another example, IT professionals installed an OA system which was integrated and offered over 100 different functions. However, a later evaluation had found that users typically accessed only 8 - 12 of the functions provided. This inevitably resulted in greatly increased overheads.

The current study suggests that the responsibility for IT investments should be divorced from the responsibilities for other investments, and should be transferred to the hands of a specially appointed executive. This person might lead a small team of key personnel drawn from different individual departments to co-ordinate all IT-related activities. The authority of the group can be assured by appointing the executive at Board level.

1.5   IS THERE A NEED FOR AN EXPLICIT IT STRATEGY?

Strategic level planning and control of vital business functions have become basic bread and butter activities for any company wishing to succeed in today's competitive markets. Comprehensive strategies for the overall mission of a company, for divisional operations, and for specific business units, are regularly formulated, updated, and amended. To achieve this, inspired vision must be combined with a variety of well-understood management practices, to the effect that medium and long-term aims, the means to achieve these aims, milestones to be reached at certain points in time, and critical success factors underpinning the overall plan, are all explicitly spelt out. This is all common management practice. The current research aimed to establish whether this practice ought to be applied equally when dealing with IT investments.

To formulate a comprehensive strategy requires hard mental work. To devise a detailed IT strategy relating to the various business and operations strategies already in place is a time and energy consuming activity. The question companies are posing to themselves is whether the corporate function of IT is important enough to justify the effort. The current research investigated that question, and further attempted to pinpoint whether there is a significant difference in the degree of difficulty experienced in a number of identified areas stemming from the introduction of IT between companies deploying IT with or without the framework of an underlying official, and explicit IT strategy.

To establish the role of IT, companies were asked how their IT involvement compares in importance with other business functions:

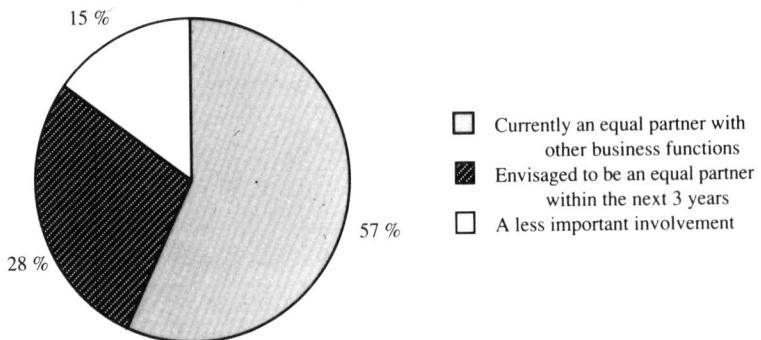

Figure 1.4 What role does IT have in your company?

- Considering that only a few years ago most companies regarded their IT involvement as no more than a backroom activity to support business conduct, the fact that 57% of companies currently rate IT on a par with other business functions, is indicative of the fact that IT has evolved from a basic supporting technology to a major enabling function which is vital to sustaining and generating business on all levels.

- A trend can be observed indicating that this figure will drastically increase and that within the next three years 85% of companies will treat IT as an equal partner with other business functions.

- It transpired that the companies treating IT as a less important involvement, 15% in the current study, did so because they were currently having their first experience with IT. As IT had not been installed for sufficiently long periods of time, it was not possible to assess its future position.

These observations are in line with figures obtained by AT Kearney in 1987 which found that 66% of companies in their sample classified IT investments as a vital or very important element in their overall business strategy.

Companies were then asked whether they introduce IT according to a well documented, explicit and company-wide strategy. The following answers were received:

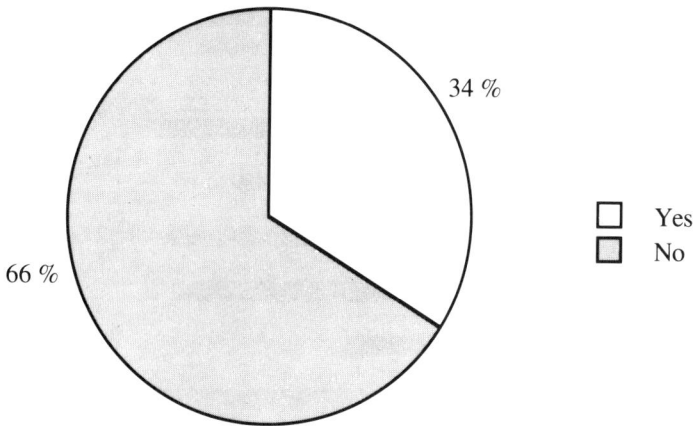

Figure 1.5 Does your company have a corporate IT strategy in place?

- Rather surprisingly, despite the importance companies attribute to IT, only a minority 34% of companies currently make the additional effort of planning their IT involvement strategically across divisions and beyond the short-term horizon.

- Additional interviews revealed that of the 66% of companies that do not have an IT strategy in place, three out of four managers declare their lack of such a strategy as an identified serious constraint to operating successfully in their chosen business field.

The results so far suggest that while IT has generally evolved into a primary business function, it is often not managed strategically in accordance with normal managerial practice.

To determine whether the presence or absence of an IT strategy shows a measurable impact on business performance, a number of potential problem areas, often arising as a consequence of the introduction of IT, have been examined for both groups:

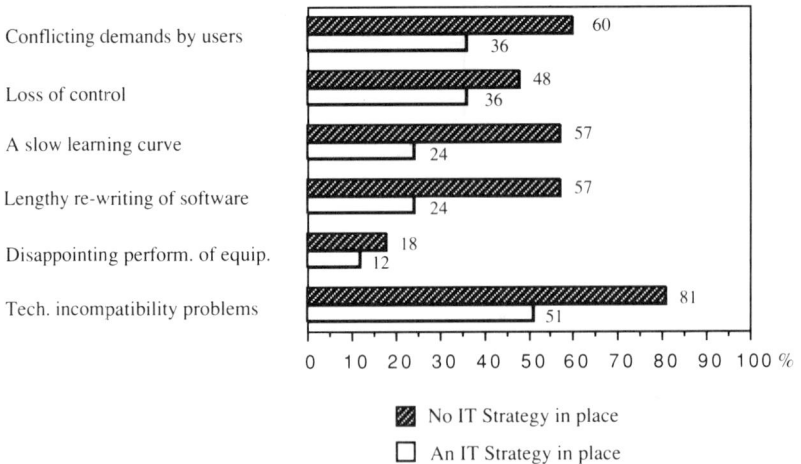

Figure 1.6 Do you experience the following difficulties?

A large cost element of introducing IT, often forgotten by many companies, is the temporary disruption to the current business. The benefits from keeping this disruption to a minimum, and therefore from saving money, can be substantial. Whereas the presence of an IT strategy does not automatically guarantee a problem-free process, it must be noted that companies with an IT strategy in place suffer considerably fewer setbacks when introducing the new technology.

A further problem observed is that traditional methods used for the costing of divisional and departmental personnel time mean that it does not pay any one division to allocate resources for the benefit of the company as a whole. Working internally will always reduce a division's profitability, and thus dampen enthusiasm for incurring a cost, when deploying appropriate personnel outside the company can produce a profit. Without top-down guidance and a defined IT strategy, it is very difficult for any one division to strive towards corporate success rather that towards divisional advantage.

Discussions with companies lacking a strategically planned approach to IT investments reveal that the absence of a corporate IT strategy is often noted to lead to:

- a loss of central control as individual divisions work out their own IT strategies, often striving towards incompatible aims

- the danger that controversial issues and problems surrounding a company's IT investments can become catalysts to separating parts of the organisation from each other

- a general view which regards IT as a technological issue where important decisions are delegated downwards, with the result that senior management subsequently has to waste considerable time and effort to regain control of IT investment decisions which do not align with top-level directions

- a method of evaluating new initiatives purely with respect to the benefit of individual divisions, even if these benefits are counterproductive to the company as a whole

- a piecemeal approach to IT where individual systems are first developed in divisional isolation, and then submitted for cross-divisional integration which, if possible at all, will often be a costly and time-consuming process

- an increased risk that local systems will be incompatible with the future plans of the organisation

- unsound data security arrangements in various information pockets of the company due to the lack of professional guidance and common standards

- unsound training arrangements and vastly different levels of user involvement

- duplication of efforts across different departments, where lessons learnt in one department are not being made available to other development teams

- general difficulties in containing the costs of the overall IT involvement due to waste, redundancy, and shorter life-cycles of systems.

Evidence that the presence of an IT strategy not only saves money, time and effort in minimising short-term teething problems, but also has a beneficial effect upon long-term business success, has been obtained by in-depth case studies at the Kobler Unit. These reveal that having a comprehensive IT strategy in place ensures that:

- the significance of pursuing medium to long-term goals instead of concentrating exclusively on short-term benefits is appreciated at all levels

- IT policies and business priorities are decided by the same managers who best understand and steer the company's overall business direction

- strategic IT plans are decided upon before setting divisional business strategies that depend increasingly on IT support

- a framework is given which allows the planning of the whole information systems portfolio, rather than the planning of individual systems in isolation

- the efforts of divisional managers, IT professionals and users, are channelled towards a common aim

- corporate core systems are planned on a common hardware/software platform and link-up with systems used by individual divisions

- resources to implement and manage corporate IT are allocated in a considered way, cutting across both divisions and the annual budget cycle

- training and user involvement are planned consistently across every level of the company

- mistakes are reduced as the infrastructure in place allows a company to learn consistently from its good and bad experiences.

It must be concluded from the current study that IT is best treated not as a technical but as a managerial issue, that has to be approached with the same basic managerial tools as any other vital business function. The weight of the evidence strongly suggests that only a comprehensive IT strategy can unify and direct efforts on all levels and across all boundaries. It must further be concluded that having an IT strategy in place has now become a prerequisite for successful business practice. Without an IT strategy, it has been shown that a number of identified problems are likely to arise which, if left unchecked, will eventually lead to a general loss of control over a wide range of IT investments.

1.6 DOES IT OFFER STRATEGIC ADVANTAGES?

The promises made by IT suppliers and technology professionals about IT have at times entered the realms of science fiction. The effect of the constant hype has been that management expectations have been raised to unrealistic levels. In particular, the belief has developed that investments in ever more powerful technology can give a company an edge on how to strategically outmanoeuvre its competitors, the means to secure a greater market share, and the ability to create continuous business growth. To support such a view, a number of well-known international case studies are quoted (American Airlines, Thomson Holidays, Dun & Bradstreet, McKesson, American Hospital Supply Corporation, and others), where the application of IT has had exceptionally high pay-backs, and where IT has been shown to have had a strategic impact upon the way in which whole markets have developed. A number of companies have tried to duplicate such success, often hoping that investing in IT will remove many of their marketing problems. However, as a rule, this has not happened and management is increasingly concerned about the value of such tactics.

The current study has found that the question on the minds of senior managers is whether the initiators responsible for such change, and for footing the bill for researching and developing the new systems, are indeed able to defend their market lead over long periods of time, and thereby able to sustain the strategic advantages gained, and with it, the profits promised.

If IT allowed companies to create sustainable strategic advantages, how could this advantage be translated into tangible benefits? What if other companies, often advised by the same consultants and using the same technology, are banking on gaining the very same leverage to increase business?

Opinions collected indicate that managers are finding it increasingly difficult to believe that technology alone is a builder of sustainable competitive advantage. All IT applications can be copied by competitors and, consequently, innovative ideas for generating better services cannot be protected. The current study found it impossible to identify any company which was able to sustain a strategic lead from any particular application of IT over more than 12 months. It is suggested that the strategic use of IT is reminiscent of the kind of industrial innovations which generate a strong impact and often substantial short-term benefits, but cannot be protected over a period of time. It must therefore be concluded that it is a fallacy to expect long-term competitive advantage from individual systems, whatever their short-term strategic impact. Once the competition catches on, further advantage can only be derived by constant improvements and additional innovations.

Is it possible that the entire market could be made to expand in such a way as to sustain strategic advantage for each player in the field?

The most obvious way in which investments in IT could benefit the market as a whole is if IT somehow enables every company to produce more and to sell more. The assumption that IT leads to a general growth of productivity has, however, been shown to be a false one. Data collected by numerous researchers, for example by the OECD, strongly suggest that although computers have become ubiquitous, overall the productivity growth rates in the industrialised world have been lower between 1979 and 1986, than in the 1970s. However, taking into account the fact that simple output production figures alone do not give the whole picture, as western society continues to develop from the industrial age into the age of information handling, these figures are not as drastic as they are at first perceived. Particularly with the recent explosion of the service industries, total economic growth has to be ascertained, both by the quality of services offered, and by the quantity of products produced. Nevertheless, it must be concluded that overall IT has so far failed to provide the productivity growth explosion it once promised.

If, as the current study suggests, IT does not lead to sustainable advantages either for individual players or for the market as a whole, it might be more useful to think about IT as a strategic necessity and as a competitive requirement for business survival. Indeed, evidence suggests that the market itself determines to some extent which IT has to be deployed in order to remain in the business. For instance, in the service sector, IT has been pioneered by several companies to link retailers into a network, with the result that costs can be cut and customers can be offered faster deliveries. Any service company operating without these particular advantages gained by the application of IT, loses out both in terms of effective resource allocation, and in terms of satisfying the newly-created expectations of customers. The firm soon realises that to stay in business, it has to adopt the same kind of infrastructure as the rest of the market in which it operates.

Companies following initiators of market standards can often balance their short-term losses against gains in diminished research and development costs. By learning from the possible mistakes of their competitors, and with the falling cost of processing power, a company will find it less expensive to install the necessary systems.

To regard IT as a strategic necessity for whole market sectors rather than as a strategic advantage for individual companies, opens up the possibility that traditional competitors could collaborate to cut the costs of researching and developing a basic IT infrastructure suitable for the particular needs of the market in which they operate. Such a joint investment would have the advantage that IT resources could be pooled, and that an industry standard could be created which would facilitate speedy development of the necessary systems. A further advantage would be that companies would not be side-tracked into competing technological avenues, but would be free to develop their own individual strengths based on unique assets, products and services. And, last but not least, from the point of view of the customer, such developments are to be hoped for, as they would minimise the disruptive effects of making the transition from an old to a new infrastructure.

CHAPTER 2

THE TRUE BUSINESS POTENTIAL OF IT

The philosophy developed by the Kobler Unit to guide practice towards the realisation of the true business potential of IT, draws a distinction between how well a company succeeds in optimising its internal organisation, and how well that company succeeds in operating within its external market environment. The opportunities that IT offers are then assessed not from the point of view of technological wizardry and sophistication but from the point of view of how IT is successfully harnessed to improve both a company's efficiency in getting the job done with a minimum of waste, and a company's effectiveness in selling its products, and of building up a loyal and expanding customer base. Furthermore, a distinction is drawn between the application of IT to fortify a company's current market position and the development of innovative IT products and IT-facilitated products to capture and create entire new market areas.

The distinction drawn between these areas emphasises the need for an approach to IT investments which is based on the parallel but distinct demands of the business. The current research has found a difference between successful and less successful companies, depending on the approach and emphasis adopted for developing the overall IT portfolio. The hallmark of best practice has been shown to be the ability of management to address these different business aims simultaneously through a well-balanced strategy of appropriate IT deployment. The characteristic of less successful practice has been found to be a strategy that concentrates on developing IT investments in a single area to the exclusion of the others; the attitude is then taken that success with IT can only be achieved through graduating from one area to the next. Thus a tendency has been observed for some companies, in the early stages of introducing IT, to justify the investment in terms of efficiency gains, later on in terms of effectiveness gains and, having grown more mature in their use of IT, in terms of developing new markets. However, case studies have shown that this is a limited investment strategy which seriously restricts the true business potential of IT.

Figure 2.1 illustrates some examples of IT applications that have been successfully developed by companies taking part in the current study, to support their individual business aims in the areas of improving internal efficiency, enhancing external effectiveness, and developing new markets:

Potential Market Environment
aim: capturing and creating new markets

Current Market Environment
aim: enhancing external effectiveness

Company Structures and Procedures
aim: improving internal efficiency

Examples of applications
• document processing
• desk top publishing
• spreadsheets
• financial reporting
• electronic mail
• project planning software
• inventory control
• skills database
• just in time manufacturing
• electronic data interchange

Examples of applications
• customer databases
• marketing databases
• help desks
• communication links with customers
• point of sale
• advertising monitoring systems
• management information systems

Examples of applications
• smart cards
• market intelligence databases
• R & D databases
• econometric modelling
• expert systems
• dealer support systems

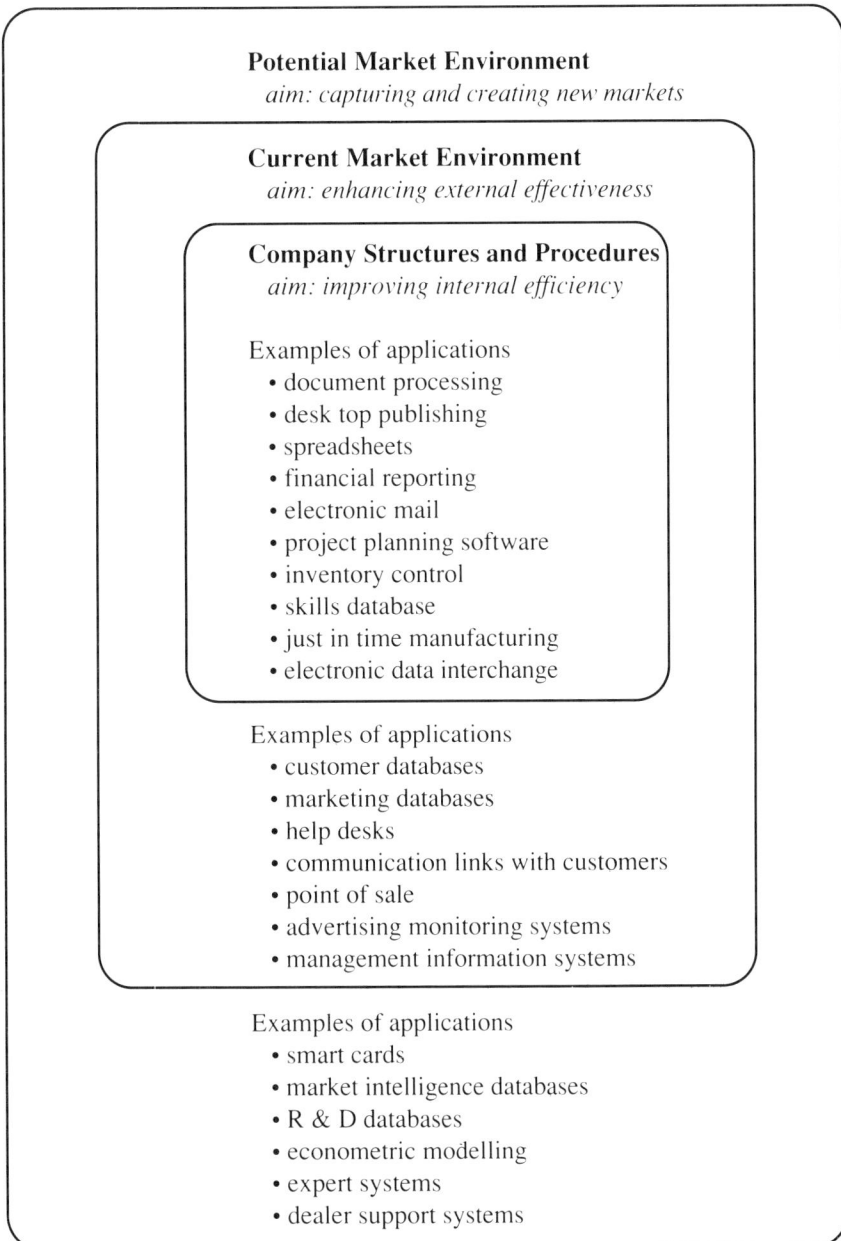

Figure 2.1 The true business potential of IT

The aim of improving internal efficiency is achieved by directing IT investments towards the optimisation of a company's infrastructure support, its management of scarce resources, its handling of repetitive tasks, its reduction of unit costs, and its internal information flow up and down the corporate hierarchy and between functions. This results in efficiency benefits for the individual, the department, and the overall company. Individuals benefit from a variety of IT applications, for instance word-processing, desk-top publishing or spreadsheeting. Facilities like project planning software, inventory control, accountancy software, and report generation packages provide valuable tools for departmental operations. Corporate efficiency can be improved through imaginative use of integrated skills and product databases, electronic mail, just-in-time manufacturing, and electronic data interchange.

Many IT applications well suited to bring efficiency benefits are readily available as off-the-shelf packages, often requiring only minimal adaptation. Such investments are critical to remaining competitive. They concentrate on basic cost cutting, but do not significantly alter or leverage other elements of the business and do not therefore create a competitive advantage. The key point is that it becomes a competitive disadvantage not to have them working optimally. However, applications directed to this area can also influence the internal structure of a company by introducing new responsibility levels and lines of communication. As a result traditional reporting structures and work procedures will change and a company will have to respond to these changes if the full benefits of IT are to be realized.

The aim of enhancing external effectiveness is achieved by directing IT investments towards optimising a company's market impact, its customer loyalty and its relationship with suppliers. A company's position within its current market environment can be enhanced and fortified through the utilisation of customer and marketing databases, help desks, communication links with both customers and suppliers, point-of-sale facilities, advertising monitoring systems, and management information systems. These provide a company with the necessary capability for introducing better customer services, for sharing customer knowledge more effectively across all departments, for cross-divisional selling, for tightening the relationship with suppliers, and for monitoring market needs.

Many IT applications well suited to bring effectiveness benefits can be developed using modern application generators. A number of such packages provide a wide range of facilities, but they require some rudimentary programming skills to generate screen layouts and to install systems suitable for a company's specific purpose. However, it has often been the imaginative use of this type of readily-available technology that has led to the development of new customer services, to new ways of doing business, even to changing industry norms. For instance, the well-documented holiday booking systems currently in use have grown out of using application generators. Similarly, deploying effective customer databases is much facilitated by using modern packages.

The aim of developing new markets is achieved through investments being directed towards using IT in an innovative way. Applications such as smart cards, market intelligence databases, econometric modelling, dealer support systems, expert systems, and R & D databases, emphasise the use of IT to differentiate the company and the quality of its service or product by offering something that did not previously exist. An example is that the development of smart cards opens up the opportunity of offering a new product, as well as the possibility of additional customer services on the back of the original investment. Investments channelled in this way may alter fundamentally the way in which the business has traditionally been conducted. In a few instances, e.g. global trading, the introduction of innovative IT applications have led to changes in the way whole industry sectors operate.

While developing innovative IT products is a high risk investment, it is a business strategy that offers the potential of high financial rewards. By introducing facilities, services and opportunities that were not possible before, new customer needs can be created. These new needs can then be fulfilled by finding ways of applying the products to advantage. Successful companies in that area state that, given appropriate risk analysis techniques, their ability to maintain a continuing commitment to the introduction of innovative IT products which have the potential to expand current market horizons, is a major ingredient contributing to their future business success.

It is realised, however, that the division of IT opportunities into three distinct areas is not absolute, and that many information systems cross these boundaries. An example is the use of project databases which increase both internal efficiency and external effectiveness. While the customer gains from obtaining more accurate planning and timescale predictions, the company gains from deploying resources more efficiently. IT applications that cross boundaries and result in both internal and external benefits improve the economics of scale or the economics of scope.

Improving the economics of scale denotes the ability to increase turnover with the same level of resources - either by extending the overall range of business transactions or by speeding up the business cycle. For instance, by introducing applications to remove bottlenecks in order-processing, or in tendering for new contracts, a company can expand its business possibilities without employing and training new staff. Improving the economics of scope denotes the ability to gain more flexibility to rapidly change products and services according to specific market needs. This will make it possible not only to offer a more individual service to different market segments, but to branch out into adjacent market areas. Some well-known examples showing that this is indeed happening can be found in the banking community, where a more personalised and effective telephone service is offered together with competitively priced services for banking-related activities like insurance cover or mortgages.

If IT can indeed be successfully exploited to improve both scale and scope - as the current case studies indicate - it follows that not only are well-established companies given exciting new possibilities to explore, but also that entirely new players in the field, particularly small firms, are given powerful tools to quickly penetrate and gain a solid foothold in a market that was previously closed to them.

To establish the areas where companies set priorities for their future investments, the following information was elicited:

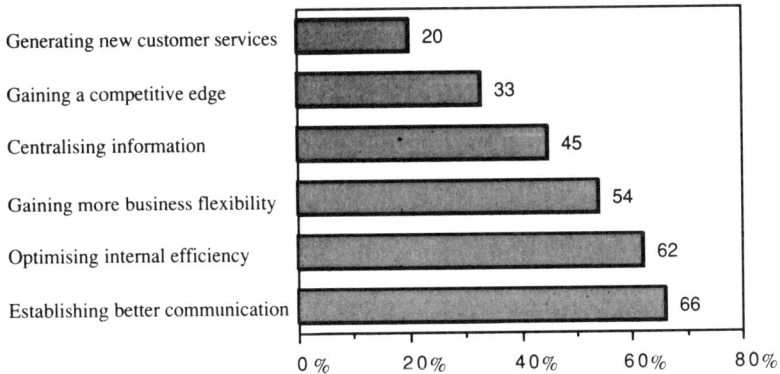

Figure 2.2 In which of the following do you place the emphasis when making further IT investments?

- The majority of managers, 66%, indicate that they are planning further investments to establish better communications. The growth of many businesses, with the subsequent opening of new offices, has increased the need for access to relevant information which is current, reliable, and timely, but not necessarily held on site in order to coordinate and manage resources optimally. As a result, investments are being geared towards facilities for increasing the speed, quality, and ease of use of currently available communication packages. Interest is particularly being shown in new developments which promise to raise traditional word processing to the realm of integrated document processing, where full documents incorporating pictures, graphs, and individual formatting can be freely exchanged across the network.

- IT investments will be directed towards optimising the internal workings of the company by 62% of managers. Besides cutting waste, managers are concerned that critical information is not readily available when needed. Often, a large amount of required data exists in isolated pockets throughout the company but is not distributed effectively. To facilitate this process, many companies plan to develop a variety of suitable databases, relationally linked to one another, so that information held by one department can be shared with other departments more easily. New horizon technology promises that Distributed Database Management systems will soon be commonplace, with the result that staff will be able to access information on their desk-tops without knowing where or how that information is physically stored.

- Gaining more business flexibility through IT investment is the aim of 54% of managers. The erosion of barriers between different business areas has made it critical for managers to expand their capacity to change the emphasis of the business at relatively short notice, as the market demands. IT investments are being geared towards overcoming restrictions imposed by traditional boundaries between functions and to improve resource allocations within and across divisions. Gaining more business flexibility has recently become a high priority business aim, as the market environment is increasingly in a state of change and as competitor response is accelerating in dynamics and strength.

• For 45% of managers, future IT investments will be directed towards centralising information for management decision-making. Many companies complain that management suffers either from information overload or from information starvation. Managers are counting on IT to provide a multi-layered information infrastructure where access to relevant information can be more easily controlled. It is realised that there is a fine balance to be struck between introducing massive centralised infrastructure systems for holding company-wide data, and smaller systems holding information necessary for operating at the front end of the business.

• Investments in IT for gaining a competitive edge are being sought by 33% of managers. For many companies the definition of competitive edge is very broad. It applies to investments aimed at ensuring that the business is not at a competitive disadvantage, as well as to investments that introduce a form of advantage. Given proper IT evaluation procedures, and a realistic assessment of the abilities of competitors to catch up, even short-term leads on competitors are considered worth achieving through clever deployment of IT.

• With only 20% of companies indicating that they are planning further investments specifically aimed at gaining customer benefits, this is the area of lowest priority for managers. Often the introduction of more customer information and 'help desk' facilities is a response to customer demands to assist more effectively with problems and enquiries.

The overall response has shown that when comparing the areas of highest and lowest priority to the three main business aims (improving internal efficiency, enhancing external effectiveness, and developing new markets) the emphasis for future investments is strongly slanted towards gaining internal efficiency.

Managers' strong commitment to directing further IT investments towards improving internal efficiency indicates their concern that organisations are not currently running optimally and that support for internal functions is not yet adequate. Expectations of what computers can offer should, however, be linked to achievable objectives. Case studies have shown that many companies hope that the introduction of sophisticated IT can help solve their basic problems of outdated structures and processes. For instance, the belief that efficiency can be improved by introducing electronic systems as a complete alternative to paper-based systems still persists, and some companies are continuing to aim for the 'paperless office', despite the mounting evidence that the introduction of computers actually increases paper consumption. Experience has shown that IT has a 'magnifying glass' effect which shows up more clearly the real strengths and weaknesses of a company's general approach. The lesson to be learnt is that before IT is introduced to improve efficiency, a company has to streamline and simplify its internal operations, often with the benefit that efficiency will be improved even before IT is introduced.

Developing the external effectiveness of a company is regarded as a low priority activity. Seeking innovative ways to serve customers better through the use of IT is an area where great scope exists for establishing benefits that can be individual to each company. The lack of commitment to directing IT towards enhancing a company's external impact has developed as a result of the difficulty of measuring, in immediate financial terms, the payback from these types of longer-term investments. This study has found that the majority of companies do not ask their customers what they need or how best the company can direct resources to meet these needs.

The potential for learning customer needs and effectively relaying them back to main offices has yet to be fully exploited. Doing so can save costs in the long run. Research carried out by the Technical Assistance Institute Research Program in the United States has shown that out of every 27 dissatisfied customers, 26 will remain uncomplaining and one will be vocal. One unhappy customer tells 12 people on average and 91% of these people will never buy from the company again. 87% will remain loyal, providing active measures are taken to solve the problems quickly. The research concludes that on average it costs a company five times more to win a new customer than it does to keep an existing one. Statistics like this show that companies cannot afford to lose the loyalty of their current customers.

Developing new markets is taken more seriously. A majority of companies are counting on IT to help them to adapt, switch, or expand the business as conditions demand. However, case studies show that there is still enormous potential for the further utilisation of IT to create and satisfy new customer needs, and to generate new business through the exploitation of innovative IT products.

The almost exclusive concentration of IT investments on gaining internal efficiency indicates that there is room for developing a more balanced investment strategy. Current practice is tilted towards achieving one aim at the expense of the others. There is still immense scope for companies to obtain a better return from their investments by shifting some of the emphasis to achieving external benefits for customers and to carving out new markets.

Indeed, if individual IT applications are planned and introduced on the basis of a corporate IT strategy, planning for overall compatibility and medium to long-term business success, it can be seen that partial development directing IT efforts to one area to the exclusion of others is an evolutionary path leading to the waste of resources, loss of control, and to a poor payback from the IT investment.

2.1   IMPROVING INTERNAL EFFICIENCY

Directing IT towards improving internal efficiency offers companies opportunities for strengthening the classic feedback loop between policy-making at the board level, the execution of policy at the operations level, the evaluation of operations and the final reintroduction of such evaluation to the policy-making part of the organisation.   As a result, the responsiveness of top management in an organisation can be increased.   By utilising IT in an imaginative way, waste can be cut, inefficiencies in allocating resources can be avoided, and a company's discretionary supporting functions can be reduced.   The ability of managers to manage, coordinate and direct both personnel and work efficiently will determine the extent of divisional and cross-divisional gains made, and the degree of added value given to the chain of internal functions and processes.   The criterion for establishing the degree of internal efficiency is management's ability to operate optimally within the company.   This is measured in terms of the extent and the strength of a company's core activities which directly support salient business objectives.

To establish the extent to which IT opportunities for improving internal efficiency are currently translated into actual business benefits, the following information was elicited:

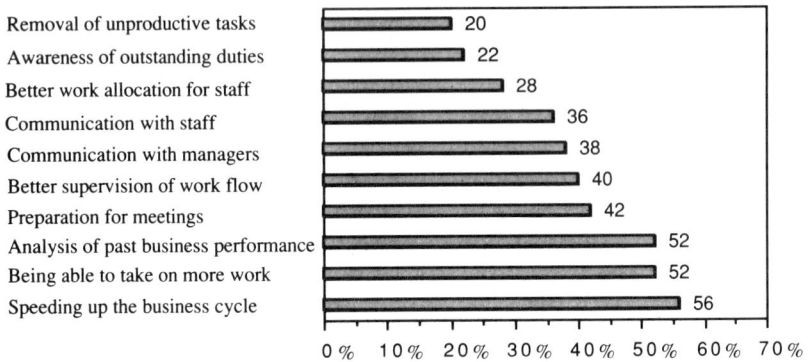

Task	Percentage
Removal of unproductive tasks	20
Awareness of outstanding duties	22
Better work allocation for staff	28
Communication with staff	36
Communication with managers	38
Better supervision of work flow	40
Preparation for meetings	42
Analysis of past business performance	52
Being able to take on more work	52
Speeding up the business cycle	56

Figure 2.3 How does IT help you to improve internal efficiency?

- The exploitation of IT to extend the economics of scale by enabling companies to speed up the business cycle (56%) and to take on more work with the same level of resources (52%) has become a widespread benefit for the majority of managers. Some companies have successfully integrated distributed databases to the point where electronic data interchange becomes possible. As a result, data is only input into the system once, even if the system is located on several sites. For instance, if a product is sold and if that information is input into an electronic sales ledger, the product is then automatically deducted from the current stock. If the current stock ledger is consequently reduced beneath a critical level, the item is then automatically reordered by adding it to a relevant ordering ledger. This obviously saves time and frees valuable company resources, both in manpower and in stock, which can be redeployed towards the task of securing additional business.

- IT has enabled a better analysis of past business performance for 52% of managers. However, it is generally acknowledged that IT offers great potential in this area and that it ought to be exploited more comprehensively. The current constraint, identified by many companies, is *the* lack of time and low priority attached to analysis and long term business planning, because these are non-fee-paying activities. Nevertheless, a large number of managers have reported that more resources ought to be allocated for the comparison of past business performance with current performance and with the performance of competitors. The ability to assess the company's position in relation to the broader market is becoming more critical as the pressures to retain current market share and current customers intensifies and becomes an active rather than a passive aim.

- For 42% of managers, IT has facilitated the preparation for meetings. IT made it possible to access comprehensive client, customer and supplier information at short notice so that managers are more aware of current negotiations, of contact with that party elsewhere in the company, and of any problems that might have arisen in the past. There is a strong feeling within all companies that even more extensive and reliable systems and information on clients and suppliers would be immensely valuable to the way in which the business operates.

- Better supervision of work flow has been reported by 40% of managers. In particular, projects can now be undertaken involving several divisions working in parallel. Omissions and slippage in timescale can be monitored more effectively, so that problems can be addressed sooner and original deadlines can be met.

- Communications both with staff (36%) and with other managers (38%) have been facilitated through the use of IT. However, Office Automation remains a contentious issue and many companies express a note of caution about attempts to structure communication too rigidly around currently available interfaces and functions of OA systems. In particular, the experience of different companies as regards the introduction of e-mail varies considerably. E-mail systems seem to be successful only in those companies where leadership from the top has laid down clear guidelines about the use of the system, and where everyone is committed and has access to the same system. Where companies do not enforce a company-wide IT strategy, there is the danger that differing systems are introduced in separate divisions of the company, leading to possible future incompatibility problems. It was found that in some companies, communications systems introduced for closer contacts with clients and customers had gradually become part of an internal communication system that was not compatible with a company system already in place elsewhere. Even though bridges between different systems exist, there is uncertainty about the transfer of formatted text and graphical information. The lack of a standard system also presents problems when employees, used to operating one system, are deployed on cross-divisional projects where another system has been installed.

The security of information sent on such 'open' systems is a further risk and problem. For some companies the type of information that can be transmitted is restricted to such a degree that it is necessary for personnel to leave the sites where they are working on a regular basis, in order to report back in person. Most companies restrict the type of information that can be accessed on OA systems, and rely heavily on a combination of other forms of communications such as telephone, fax, telex or personal courier.

- IT has contributed to achieving better work allocation for 28% of managers and enabled a greater awareness of outstanding duties to be performed by 22%. The particular systems introduced have focused specifically on resource planning and control programs. These have enabled managers to track and deploy their departmental resources better, with the result that duplication of processes has been avoided and current work priorities have been more quickly identified.

- IT has facilitated the removal of unproductive tasks for 20% of managers. This has been achieved mainly by installing improved communication lines which cut out intermediate authorisations, and by replacing the need for a number of laborious but previously necessary revisions of documents and letters.

Overall, the success with which IT has been exploited to improve efficiency varies considerably. The extensive use of PCs has meant that individual managers now introduce IT more rapidly into their divisions. However, experience has shown that this is often not coordinated across departments and that it leads to possibilities of future incompatibility. Earlier research by the Kobler Unit report found that some 20% of managers interviewed did not personally make use of IT. This emphasis has now changed, both as a result of the flexibility and increasing user-friendliness of systems, as well as the increasing necessity for managers to take control of the flow of information, and the resulting need to be connected to their own divisional or company networking system.

The current research has found that it is not possible to produce a straightforward automation of orthodox communication. Trying to do so raises both social and organisational issues. The introduction of electronic systems forces users, to restructure deep-rooted habits of communication in very fundamental ways. The problems associated with doing this are still evident in companies, particularly where systems are introduced which do not facilitate the way people work. If internal communication is to be improved, processes and systems have to be introduced that are directed towards the aims of the users rather than forcing users to change their ways in order to compensate for the deficiencies in the equipment. Companies must be willing to spend more time on analysing the needs of users before allocating funding to IT which may not always be the most appropriate solution.

Previous Kobler Unit research has shown that companies agree that the introduction of IT has to be accompanied by the simplification of existing procedures, processes and functions. To implement this is not easy, and often different managers even within the same company cannot agree about the exact level of restructuring needed. This dilemma still exists for management today. However, a few companies can point to some successful reorganisation of corporate and divisional reporting structures by exposing more surface to their external environment.

There is a lack of willingness on the part of top management to allocate sufficient time, funding and personnel to overcoming internal problems associated with the introduction and management of IT. The identified concentration of IT investments aimed at achieving internal efficiency does not provide the solution to this problem, unless adequate planning, commitment, and thought are also invested. Without a change in managements' priorities it will become increasingly difficult to retain control of the internal developments and changes which are produced by the introduction of IT.

2.2   ENHANCING EXTERNAL EFFECTIVENESS

Directing IT towards enhancing external effectiveness offers companies opportunities for securing market share by adding value to existing services and products. As customer expectations rise, sensitivity to market needs and knowledge of competitors become crucial.   IT can help address these requirements. Particularly, IT holds the potential for making it possible to replace the era of mass marketing by personalising services and by directing new products and services to precisely-defined market segments. The criterion for establishing the degree of external effectiveness is a company's ability to satisfy customer demands. This is measured in terms of the strength of a company's marketing intelligence, its quality of products and services, its speed of response to enquiries and orders, and its success in tying customers to the company.

To establish the extent to which IT opportunities for enhancing external effectiveness are currently translated into actual business benefits, the following information was elicited:

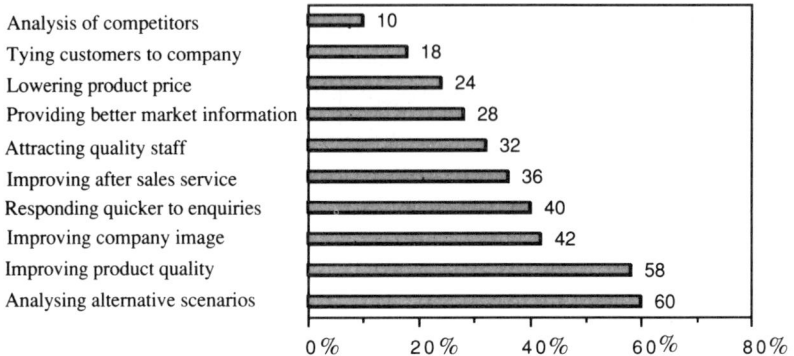

Figure 2.4 How does IT help you to enhance external effectiveness?

• The majority of managers, 60%, have found 'what if' computations an essential tool for obtaining management advantage through providing future scenario predictions of business strengths and weaknesses. Those companies not utilising 'what if' computations to advantage have highlighted the problems they have in gaining access to specific information about projects to which they are already committed. Increasingly, companies want detailed information about projects, such as individual man costs, and often the information does not exist in a readily accessible form.

- A strong application of IT is made in the area of improving product quality, as stated by 58% of managers in the study. For many companies this has shown itself most clearly in improved standards ranging from better quality of letters, reports and graphical information, to more detailed product specifications, and to an increased quality and range of international trading arrangements. The large-scale application of IT to this area of the business has to an extent been set by the rapid development of the market. As many businesses have begun to be affected, they have been forced to introduce a certain level of IT in order to remain competitive. This is particularly true of global trading operations, design, manufacturing, architectural and engineering consultancy work.

- Responding quicker to customer enquiries has resulted in business benefits, as reported by 40% of managers. The evidence for this is that companies can indicate a quicker response time to answering enquiries and dealing with orders, more detailed and accurate accounting systems, better payment facilities with electronic funds transfer, improved lead times, and smoother ordering systems. Just-in-time manufacturing systems are beginning to be more widely used, not only in heavy manufacturing industries but also in retailing. The introduction of automatic quoting systems for giving guide-line pricing for different configurations of products has also produced marked improvements in confirmed ordering for some companies. Furthermore, IT has been found to be useful in the scheduling of work plans and in allowing last-minute customer requirements to be introduced and incorporated into proposals. IT has become indispensable in that it has allowed work to be carried out on several different sites, which is then compiled into the formal submission in time to meet the pre-set deadlines.

- The necessity of using IT for improving the company image (42%) and for attracting quality staff (32%) has been acknowledged. Every single company interviewed was concerned with the possibility of encountering problems in future staff recruitment. It is further acknowledged that there is an increasing expectation, particularly amongst younger staff, that employees should have sophisticated IT facilities at their disposal. Attracting and retaining more quality staff is an important business aim for most companies, particularly in the light of the expected fall in the number of school leavers and graduates and the predicted downturn in experienced personnel available for work. Some managers already regard their businesses as people-constrained, but there is still unwillingness in many companies to provide well-planned and thought-out training on a regular basis. Simply establishing an IT image will not guarantee, in the long term, that staff recruitment becomes easier during the expected shortage, nor will it, by itself, increase a company's ability to retain qualified staff.

- Currently, 36% of company managers find in IT an essential tool for improving after-sales services, but only 18% of managers have used IT to strengthen the links with their customers. Given that these are areas of increasing importance in a competitive market, it seems that there is room for improvement. The need to regard after-sales service and customer contact as an expected and therefore essential part of the product or service is only very gradually being appreciated. For instance, customer records showing the history of contacts between company departments and customers could be made available, to be accessed electronically across the whole company. This would facilitate regular client contacts and could provide a basis for informing specific clients about relevant new information, as updates of products or new services are made available. IT can also assist considerably when dealing with new enquiries from old customers. It is questionable, in some companies, whether data available to the individual departments is managed and used to best effect for the exploitation of business advantage. There is room for greater appreciation and use of this asset.

- IT investments have led to the provision of better information about the market for 28% of managers while only 10% of managers identified IT as having assisted in the analysis of competitors. Some firms, however, have experimented with sales management systems which coherently capture customer feedback on new product launches, and channel that information back to the marketing department. A knowledge of how the market in general is evolving and how competitor companies in particular are reacting to or determining the market, provides a secure basis upon which to operate in a chosen field.

- Lowering the product price through the use of IT has been possible for 24% of managers. Essentially, this has been achieved through optimising IT investments by gaining the benefits of economy of scale, both in terms of speed of production and in terms of unit costs. The consequence of a speeded-up production cycle is that time costs can be reduced, and this is reflected in the end product or service price.

During the current study it was noted that the majority of managers are unable to give precise definitions of their exact information needs. As a result, IT systems in use offer a wide range of information that is often of varying quality and relevance. Without better definition of information needs, the full potential of current IT investments will continue not to be fully realised. IT has not yet been effectively and comprehensively harnessed for the analysis of competitors, market conditions, and customer information. The reluctance of managers to apply IT to these areas suggests a lack of a structured framework within which both long-term business objectives are established and short-term efforts are spelt out.

Although management's awareness of the need to establish stronger links with their customers is very high, the translation of this awareness into reality has not, however, been so successful. Management is hesitant about investing for long-term objectives, particularly when they are related to external aspects of the company, such as improved customer support and after-sales service. There are still weaknesses in the quality of the company/customer relationship, particularly in knowing and understanding the customers and in the perception of the aims they pursue and the services they require. Mainly due to the lack of a unified effort and market standards, the potential of linking a company's information systems directly to the systems that customers operate has hardly been exploited. If management wants to compete successfully in increasingly international markets and take up the opportunities IT offers to enhance effectiveness, deep-rooted attitudes based on isolation and on neglecting quality and customer support will have to give way to the willingness to form partnerships on all fronts, but particularly with a company's most important asset - its customers.

2.3   DEVELOPING NEW MARKETS

Directing IT towards developing new markets offers companies opportunities for long-term future business success by enhancing both the scale and scope of their services, by creating secure niche positions, and by introducing services and products that did not previously exist. This can be achieved by exploiting the versatility of already installed systems to make inroads into adjacent markets, or by the clever handling of innovative technology to create and satisfy entirely new customer needs. On a larger scale, IT offers opportunities for making information handling itself a marketable commodity.

The already extensive deployment of IT in many companies has provided opportunities for changing the way many businesses have traditionally operated. The costs encountered in installing and running IT have prompted companies to look around for ways of recovering some of their initial outlay. Primarily, this has been achieved through maximising the use made of information already held and by making improved use of existing systems to introduce new income-generating services. This has increased capacity handling and flexibility, and has led to a situation where it is now possible to utilise a company's resources to become a serious player in new but related areas of business. As a result, the once clearly defined barriers between many different business areas have come under pressure or ceased to exist.

Adjacent markets have been captured in three particular ways. Firstly, a company can simply acquire either one of their suppliers or one of their distributors, and then use IT to glue the whole operation together. This will lead to stronger control over the production to sale cycle. It is most successfully achieved where links between two companies already exist. For instance, a number of car manufacturers have secured access to their customers by buying showrooms and establishing dealerships with direct on-line ordering to the factory. Similarly, many building societies have established contact with their potential borrowers earlier in the house purchasing chain by buying up estate agencies and by linking the two businesses with IT.

The second way in which to move into adjacent markets is where a company has expanded its business without actually buying up the associated services, but by forging partnerships with separate but related companies in order to offer customers a more attractive deal. The experience of airlines providing hotel bookings world-wide or fly-drive deals, has become so established that it is no longer considered exceptional. Car hire and car rescue organisations are able to offer their members an increasingly wide range of specially negotiated deals, such as travel discounts and reduced insurance rates, using their favourable position in the market and their previously collected membership or client details to gain direct access to customers at appropriate times.

The third possibility existing for moving into adjacent markets is where a company has exploited the dormant facilities of already installed IT systems to extend the range of services that it is able to offer to its customers. The industry-wide extension of banking into the provision of mortgages and insurance services illustrates how completely an adjacent business area, can be supported by imaginative application of IT. Based on the expectation that bank customers are also likely to be house buyers and to need insurance cover, existing information can be used to provide a more specific, tailored service. This has provided the banks with an advantageous line of business and an additional source of income.

Once one company successfully begins to make the strategic move into an adjacent business area it puts pressure on its competitors to follow. Furthermore, it forces companies in the threatened fields to review their own market security and position as the real threat develops of their being cut out of the original business area. New lines of competition are created as the emphasis shifts from the traditional areas to the unknown. The restructuring of whole business sectors may result. This redefinition of business can be particularly dramatic as, for instance, has been the restructuring necessary in the City, leading up to the Big Bang.

In addition to moving into adjacent business areas, the development of innovative IT products can be directed towards developing entirely new markets by creating and satisfying new customer needs. For instance, the development of automatic teller machines has led to the existence of 24-hour banking facilities. The development of home banking has similarly become possible through technology. One building society has achieved nationwide coverage and a near monopoly in electronic banking through the use of viewdata and TV sets. Customers can pay bills, obtain computer-approved loans, and check their accounts at all times from the comfort of their home. According to the Chief Executive this has created a unique monopolistic service outside mainstream building society activity. While others are competing with identical products and similar terms, this society is attacking a new market-place.

Imaginative use of IT can also be directed towards creating new products as a sideline to the main business area. This can happen as a result of having originally developed an IT-based product in-house for internal use. A company might well find that it is possible to subsequently sell that product to other firms. For instance, the development of smart cards has led to the situation where companies whose main business may be banking, retailing or engineering, can develop smart cards not only for their own business but also as a product for their customers. As a result, a proportion of any development costs can be reclaimed and expertise in a new area can be consolidated. Similarly, the development and speedy acceptance of cellular telephones has created a massive potential market and, for the originator companies, a lucrative new business area.

These examples illustrate some of the potential for future economic expansion. While it is true that some industries are rendered obsolete by the introduction of new technological products, economic expansion is not finite or attainable only by balancing the success of some industries against the demise of others. The failure of some industries to keep pace both in technological terms and in terms of societal needs means that their products or services have been superseded by others which are more appropriate. The sustainability of any new market is the degree to which it is acceptable and useful to society. Scope exists for new products to be developed which, when harnessed to particular needs, become indispensable. In the home, for instance, IT has already enabled homeworking, home banking, and widespread telecommunications contact. Further potential exists for addressing the special needs of particular groups, for example, the elderly and the infirm by gearing IT developments to reducing their isolation and remoteness from normal life. It is now recognised that IT can be exploited to advance economic growth. For instance, a recent OECD report concludes that 'Long-term growth should be viewed as a process of matching technologies with social needs. Successful mastery of technical and social transformations brought about by the information revolution is the key to growth prospects and the future development of our societies.'

Information handling itself has become a source of market growth with immense returns. IT has provided the means for storing and accessing information, the value of which is enhanced by being delivered at speed at the critical time. The necessity for companies to have access to current market information has meant that most companies have initiated sophisticated databases. While retaining an option on first access to the data, they can obtain further business by offering access to it to others in the field. The development of on-line press services by newspaper companies and the establishment of national market intelligence databases provide two examples of this.

In education, better information handling for improving the effectiveness of current educational practices is now possible through the application of IT. The convergence of new technologies, leading to workable multimedia systems, means teachers have at their disposal additional tools for providing relevant material in a more interesting way. The introduction of IT into training and education can greatly assist teachers in addressing the needs of individual pupils, as opposed to the needs of an entire class.

Initiating a move towards developing new markets, be it by extending the business into adjacent areas, by creating and satisfying new customer needs, or by selling information products, carries with it risk. The degree of risk involved has to be weighed against the potential benefits to be gained. High risk must offer high benefits. However, it must be borne in mind that if a new business, based on innovative use of IT, is successful, it will not necessarily be possible to protect the original initiative over a long period of time. Other companies may eventually be able to follow, often more cheaply, and by avoiding possible mistakes made by the originator company, may even leap-frog the competition.

Leaving innovation to others to bear the start-up costs, and then following, also incurs certain risks. If a company leaves it too late to follow then it may be cut out of business if the other contenders have succeeded in locking in the customers. The example of Thomson Holidays successfully tying their customers, the travel agents, to their network through offering a sophisticated on-line booking and confirmation service, is well documented. However, this TOP system has now become an industry-wide standard and other tour operators have been forced to follow and to offer a similar service. Nevertheless, if the strategy is to follow, then it must be done quickly, which means knowing what the competition is doing and how the market is developing.

Despite numerous case studies demonstrating exciting opportunities to create new markets by imaginative use of IT, the current study found that many companies still neglect to develop this potentially powerful asset. The majority of companies concentrate on using IT mainly for expanding their existing business, rather than for venturing into adjacent markets, creating new customer needs, or developing their capacity to handle marketable information. When companies were asked how current IT installations have facilitated opening up new markets, only 4% of the respondents regarded IT as 'absolutely essential', and only 22% as 'very helpful'.

If a company is indeed serious about keeping pace with a world that is changing rapidly, it will have to look increasingly towards IT when aiming to enhance its flexibility to venture into new markets. What is required by management is a more committed, proactive approach, and a shift in a company's perception of what IT can do for the company - not only in terms of operating within the current business areas, but also by considering IT as the key to unlocking new markets.

CHAPTER 3

CONTROLLING IT INVESTMENTS BY ADAPTING TO CHANGE

To control IT investments, a company must adapt rapidly and learn to continue to adapt to the many changes happening concurrently in its environment. The present study has found that the profound changes in market conditions, in customer demands, in employee expectations and in available technology are all powerful forces exerting pressures on companies to protect their systems against some of the consequences of these changes. The indications are that the rate of change is accelerating and that managers are being forced to define a role for IT within business parameters that are themselves increasingly coming into question or are already collapsing. The problem for today's managers is how to direct IT investments towards a projected market when that market itself is evolving dynamically.

What has become evident is that no company can remain entirely isolated from the wave of changes occurring in today's increasingly international markets. While some managers try to remain impervious to external changes, these changes nevertheless occur, and, if disregarded, result in alienating a company from its market environment. This ultimately leads to directing new IT initiatives towards an outdated view of that environment. What is required is to design a corporate mechanism to assess the relative impact of external change on a company's IT investment, to formulate a corporate response to that change, and to protect new IT initiatives from unforeseen change.

Controlling IT investment

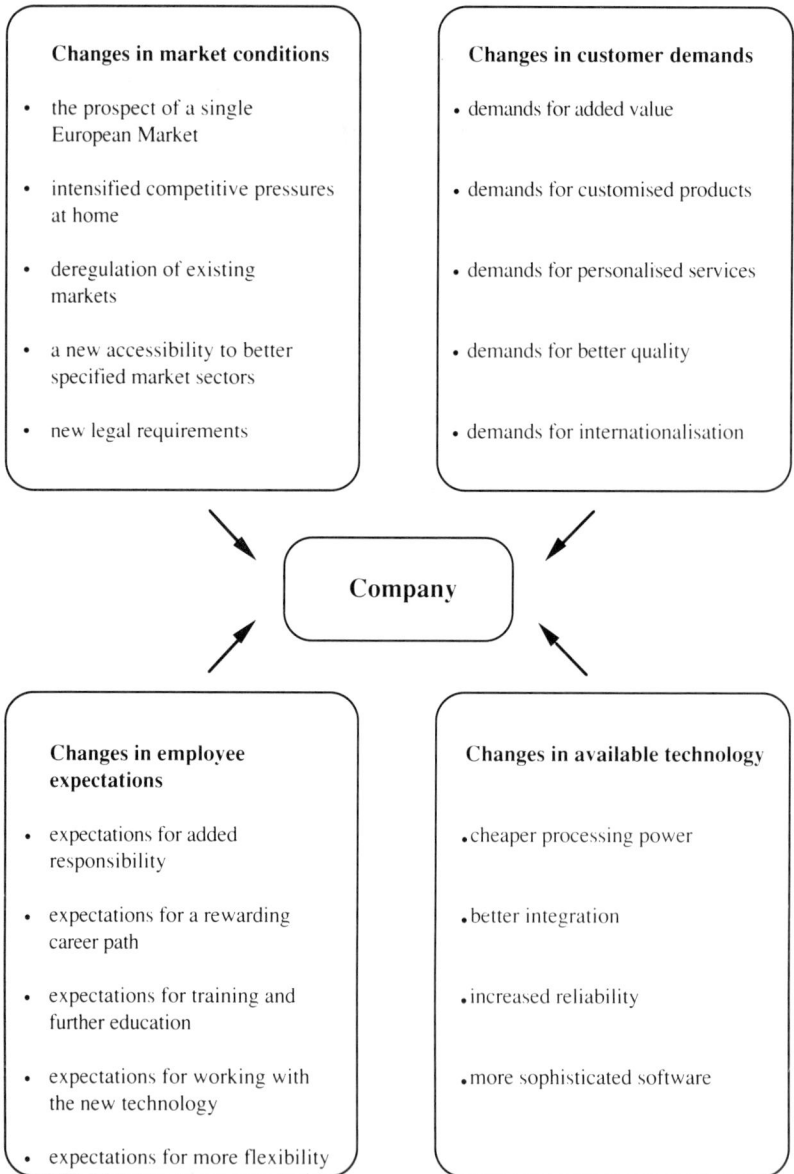

<table>
<tr><td>

Changes in market conditions

- the prospect of a single European Market

- intensified competitive pressures at home

- deregulation of existing markets

- a new accessibility to better specified market sectors

- new legal requirements

</td><td>

Changes in customer demands

- demands for added value

- demands for customised products

- demands for personalised services

- demands for better quality

- demands for internationalisation

</td></tr>
</table>

Company

<table>
<tr><td>

Changes in employee expectations

- expectations for added responsibility

- expectations for a rewarding career path

- expectations for training and further education

- expectations for working with the new technology

- expectations for more flexibility

</td><td>

Changes in available technology

- cheaper processing power

- better integration

- increased reliability

- more sophisticated software

</td></tr>
</table>

Figure 3 Controlling IT investments by adapting to change

The current study has identified national and international forces that propagate changes in market conditions, customer demands, employee expectations and available technology:

- Changing market conditions are forcing companies to devise new strategies. Relentless competition, the prospect of a single European market, sweeping deregulation, new legal requirements and a newly-found accessibility to better specified market sectors are some of the key forces propagating change in this area. Companies successfully adapting to these changes are directing new IT initiatives towards collecting and manipulating better market information, towards projecting sophisticated 'what if' scenarios in preparation for market changes and towards pinpointing selected market sectors.

- The role of the customer has recently undergone a complete reversal as his power to choose and to determine the level of service and product quality has increased. Today's customers demand better responsiveness from companies, and expect to be treated as individuals with specific requirements. Many successful companies are willing to listen to these demands, as they can no longer afford to lose customers simply because of a poor reputation. Strong communication links are forged with customers and supply lines are expanded in order to cater for the increasing internationalisation of customers. Some companies are successfully directing new IT initiatives towards adding better value to their products and towards offering a more personalised service. As a result, these companies are able to maintain and increase their customer base.

- At a time when skilled staff are considered an increasingly scarce resource, key employees expect to be treated as individuals with valuable contributions to make, and are forcing companies to devise new procedures for traditional work practices. Today's employees expect to be given a level of responsibility that mirrors their ability, to be offered a rewarding career path, and to be trained comprehensively both in IT and in business practice. Companies successfully adapting to these developments are finding that new IT initiatives can be directed towards fulfilling some of these expectations by providing suitable facilities for employees to work optimally. Furthermore, some companies are establishing appropriate databases of personnel and skills to deploy staff more effectively, and are employing sophisticated multi-media technology to speed up the training and learning process.

• Technological progress is forcing companies to keep pace with new developments. The speed of technological change, the reduction in the cost of processing power, better integration of equipment, increased reliability, and more sophisticated software offer improved information handling and determine what becomes possible and cost effective. Companies successfully adapting to these changes in technology are directing new IT investments towards exploiting new opportunities, towards taking on new initiatives, and towards doing things that were not previously possible.

Case studies have shown that there are two distinct reactions to how companies deal with change. Companies either fear change and regard it as a threat to their established way of operating, or they welcome change and regard it as an opportunity to explore new business avenues. If the perception is one of threat, new IT initiatives are directed towards achieving the familiar and towards reinforcing existing practices. If the perception is to regard change as an opportunity, further IT initiatives are being directed towards facilitating the process of change itself.

An illustrative example is the comparative experience of two organisations which both decided to deploy large-scale IT. The first company regarded change as a threat and made the decision to invest in IT in order to refine current practices by attempting to automate them. This was done by trying to encapsulate in electronic form all existing processes, information-sharing structures, variations and nuances in the normal pattern of people's work. The company did not concern itself unduly with the fact that many of the existing processes being transferred to the electronic systems were ineffective in the first place and were based on an old perception of the company's needs. The organisation was in effect reinforcing the rigidity of its already redundant procedures and was not prepared to adapt its IT investments in order to address the real problems that employees were experiencing in their daily work. The frustrations and despair of working with this system soon became obvious as the introduction of IT was seen not to be removing any of the problem areas but rather drawing them into sharper focus.

By contrast, the second company regarded change as an opportunity and made the decision to invest in IT not for purposes of automating existing processes but in order to try to expand and strengthen its position in an increasingly international market. First a thorough evaluation of current practices was conducted, and, as a result, a major restructuring of the allocation of tasks and of the definition of functions emerged. The company then directed new IT initiatives towards supporting and optimising these new working practices. Furthermore, the company launched a comprehensive programme assessing current environmental changes in its market environment. Further IT initiatives were then directed towards new windows of business opportunities. By adapting its IT investments to the flow of change already in progress and by using IT to facilitate that change, the company was able to actively support the efforts of management at all levels to operate effectively in a turbulent environment.

The distinction in philosophy between these two examples is particularly instructive. The first company is looking inwards and is using IT simply to replicate existing historical practices, without objectively assessing the relevance of these to its external and evolving market environment. The second is looking outwards, towards what it needed to achieve in order to continue being in a business that is changing rapidly and to facilitate the new ways of working that become necessary. It was trying to anticipate and accommodate change which it is unable to prevent. As a result, it adapted its IT investment in order to help create change and to transform a potential threat into an opportunity.

3.1   CHANGES IN MARKET CONDITIONS

The traditional market environment in which companies have been used to operating is undergoing fundamental and complex change. Working within market conditions that are in a constant state of flux means that the emphasis and source of the competition is also changing.   While IT itself is instrumental in enabling and propagating change in the first place, it has also become an important component for exploiting new market possibilities to the benefit of many companies.

The current study has found that the prospect of a single European market, intensification of competition, deregulation of existing markets, and a newly-found accessibility to better specified market sectors are all powerful forces bringing about change:

- The prospect of an integrated European market, although primarily based on economic considerations, has only become a practical possibility through the application of IT.   The realisation that Europe must adapt to mounting pressures generated by major developments in the world economy and in international markets has forced change upon countries and companies. Through an imaginative use of IT, a company can prepare itself to operate successfully across this wider field, particularly by exploiting IT to effectively strengthen communication links within a multi-site and multi-national business environment, by encouraging data sharing and the use of distributed databases between different locations, by a better sharing of market intelligence which currently exists only in isolated pockets, and by sustaining or increasing its overall flexibility to deploy resources effectively.

- The threat of increased competitive pressure has intensified as some companies are quick to adapt their efforts to seize new opportunities. Developments like a single European market not only offer exciting new opportunities abroad but also threaten that competition can be imported back into a company's traditional market areas. This can lead to a situation where too many firms are competing for the same customers, resulting in a company having to make concerted efforts to offer better value. As a result there has been a spate of mergers and acquisitions, in order to establish power bases and to prevent take-overs, which have transformed many market sectors. In the current study, only a small minority of companies, 10%, are already using IT to assist in analysing information about their competitors. For a company to keep pace, new IT initiatives must be adapted to this increased agility of competitors, both by adding value to its products and services, and by monitoring the developments of competitors.

- The deregulation of many markets has come about as companies press for greater flexibility and more freedom to operate effectively. This has led to the decision by many governments to loosen the regulatory controls of traditional industries so that they become responsible for their own standards and policing. Major restructuring of whole industries may result. For instance, in the City of London some radical market changes occurred leading up to the financial services deregulation referred to in the popular press as 'Big Bang'. Monopolies which once protected businesses and whole industries are being swept away, leaving many companies, once secure in their markets, open and vulnerable to competition and to change. Successful companies are exploiting the newly-found freedom of deregulation and are directing new IT initiatives towards building up an international network dealing in several markets at the same time, towards analysing the implications, threats and opportunities of deregulation, and towards projecting sophisticated 'what if' scenarios for planning further developments.

- A newly found accessibility to better specified market sectors is indicating the end of the mass market area. Companies realise this greater accessibility by pinpointing target markets more precisely and by customising products and services to better analysed individual needs. Additionally, new IT initiatives are being directed towards identifying market segments in other industries that promise business opportunities. Being better informed about market conditions allows a more effective targeting of prospective customers and obviates the need for expensive blanket promotions which often fail to attract sufficient interest and response. Those companies that successfully identify and supply their customers' specific requirements are further benefiting from sustaining a dialogue which allows the company to obtain valuable market information. This, in turn, enables the company to initiate and maintain very flexible marketing and sales strategies which are often difficult for the opposition to imitate.

Without understanding the forces that propagate change, the basic directions in which the market is so rapidly developing, and without laying an increased importance on collecting and analysing relevant market information, a company will direct its IT investment towards an image of what the market is considered to be or was, rather than the reality of what it is, and will be.

Gaining access to relevant market information can be facilitated by the use of IT, particularly by making increased use of on-line marketing databases. The present study found that while on-line marketing databases are now widely accepted, only 28% of managers use IT to collect and analyse information in-house about market developments. While the collection of such information alone does not secure access to market share, it ensures that trends and opportunities can be detected and analysed. As a result of such analyses it becomes possible to redirect a company's efforts effectively at short notice.

Overall, the current study has found that a remarkable number of strategies for deploying new IT initiatives are planned without sufficient understanding and analysis of the changes already occurring in present market conditions. Case studies strongly suggest that companies not adapting their IT investment to take account of these new developments lose control over that investment.

3.2   CHANGES IN CUSTOMER DEMANDS

During the past decade, there has been a steady increase in the number of companies offering customers a wider variety of value added products and novel services that were not previously possible. The worldwide explosion in communications, the revolution in global market conditions, the opening-up of new trade markets, intensified competition and continued deregulation have all contributed towards giving the customer more options and more choice. As a result, the power of customers has grown and their demands for better services and better products have increased. Customers are now more assertive about what are considered acceptable standards of performance and service, and are prepared to switch their loyalties to companies that will respond quickly.

Traditionally, the role and status of the customer have been fairly low down on the list of critical factors determining a company's business strategy. The perception of customers in the past has often been that they were privileged to buy from the company and that there was no company obligation to provide after-sales service or further support. In fact, many companies tended to regard their customers as a necessary nuisance. In the days where customers were less mobile and had limited choice, this attitude was tolerated because the alternatives were non-existent. As a result the lack of customer mobility was misinterpreted by many companies as signalling continuing satisfaction and sustainable customer loyalty. Interest in the customer was minimal and the larger the company grew, the more likely it was that it cushioned itself against direct customer access. This was exemplified by the role of the service departments in many companies which was often more synonymous with customer complaints than with customer service. Its role was to fend off customers and to maintain the company's remoteness, to be reactive to irritating complaints rather than proactive to customer needs.

The realisation that it is the customer who is the lifeblood of a company is only dawning slowly on many organisations. As customers, who are themselves growing to establish an international presence, now demand to be treated as individuals with their individual needs, with requirements for consistency of service and steady supply of products, many companies are now engaging in a positive effort to become more customer-oriented. For instance, while after-sales service used to be considered an extra by many companies, it is now increasingly regarded as an expected and therefore important part of the product that has to be provided. The current study has found that IT can help and that 40% of companies are using IT to facilitate the task of responding quicker to customer needs.

The current study has found that many successful companies adapt their IT investments to drive a three-stage programme designed first to identify their existing customers more accurately, then to establish an informative dialogue with identified customers, and finally to close the gap between a customer's expectations and the ability of the company to satisfy them:

- The first stage of this metamorphosis towards becoming a customer-oriented company has to be a knowledge of who exactly constitutes their customers. This seemingly simple exercise of assessment is often fraught with difficulties. It has been found in numerous marketing surveys and in the current research that many companies have only a vague idea of the profile of their customers. For instance, the majority of companies selling through agents or supplying retail outlets find it very difficult to keep track of who buys their products, or how frequently. An imaginative application of IT has enabled some companies to facilitate the task of identifying their existing customers more accurately by combining their existing databases with programs that analyse and search that data for recurring patterns.

- The second stage towards gaining a closer knowledge of the customer is to establish an informative dialogue with customers identified by collecting and manipulating data from various sources. This requires a coordinated approach to collecting additional relevant data in each division dealing directly with customers. This data then has to be structured, analysed and made available throughout the company. Often it is the experience of customers that they are unable to gain continuity of contact both over time and across a company, particularly when they deal with several different departments. The introduction of IT can help to provide that continuity and enable a company to offer a service that is individualised towards particular customers.

- The third stage involved in making a company more customer-friendly is to target IT investments towards closing the gap between a customer's expectations and the ability of the company to satisfy these expectations. Companies that fail to give satisfaction to customers in terms of speed of delivery, availability, and comprehensive after-sales service leave themselves wide open to what has been described as a 'vulnerability factor' (Aleksander, 1987). Even market leaders can be vulnerable to loss of market share when small but determined competitors are successfully directing new IT initiatives towards closing that gap. An example is the company, a long-term market leader, that was content to rely on the weight of its household name for future business success, rather than on the perception of the company by its current customers. A closer analysis revealed that over 75% of its current IT investments had been directed towards areas contributing less than 25% of the value added, hardly touching those areas where the company was most vulnerable to competitors. Hence, when new competitors directed their IT initiatives more strategically towards identifying and satisfying the expectations of customers, the market leader lost market share and customers. On the other hand, where 'help desks' have been installed, the retained goodwill and additional information that have accrued has been substantial, compared to the loss of customers sustained previously, often without the company's knowledge, until it was too late to recover the situation. The additional opportunities for enhanced cooperation between company and customer through the use of interorganisational systems have produced benefits to both as a result of increasing the speed of the business cycle.

What has become evident is that while some companies neglect their customers, others are making a decisive effort to service their customers, and that IT has become one of the most effective tools for guiding that effort. A trend can be observed where an increasing number of companies are successful in pulling together information collected by their sales staff about the preferences and habits of their customers. This enables a company to construct a better profile of its customers, thus enabling a more thorough support service to be offered. Comprehensive customer records showing the full history of contacts between company divisions/employees and customers, the enhancement of these records by inputting data specifically collected from the customer, and the effective sharing of these enhanced records across the whole company, are all essential in contributing to an efficient and effective customer service in today's fast-paced market .

A useful method for directing IT investments towards the benefits of customers can be found in the notion of the Customer Resource Life Cycle (Blake, Ives and Learmonth, 1987). The method is based around a 13-stage model that traces how customer needs change over time. It is a means of structuring the way in which a company can optimise its investments in IT in order to be of most benefit to its customers in meeting their changing requirements. The model essentially allows identification of where strategic applications of IT may be made in order to help the customer manage its own resources more effectively. It is a method of ensuring that a company remains in tune with its customers, and how through the effective use of IT a company can establish a position of supremacy on the basis of cost, enhanced service or differentiation of product. Investments channelled in this way produce direct visible benefits to both companies and their customers, while linking the two more closely together.

Overall, the current study strongly suggests that the extent to which a company is able to succeed in its market depends increasingly on its ability to react to, predict, and fulfil customer requirements through knowledge of its customers, their markets and needs. The loyalty of existing customers cannot be taken for granted, and a company has to make a positive effort to identify existing customers, to establish a continuous and extended dialogue with customers, and to learn effectively from that dialogue. If a company does not adapt its IT investment to the raised expectations of their customers, the return on that investment will be poor.

3.3   CHANGES IN EMPLOYEE EXPECTATIONS

Operating in the current environment of change demands a new sophistication and an approach which facilitates continuous adaptation.   A result of external dynamic factors is that expectations of both companies towards their employees, and of employees towards their companies are raised.   Companies now insist that employees should be prepared to work with technology, as the use and manipulation of information becomes an increasingly large component of most jobs, that they should be ready to accept broader responsibilities in line with changing job structures, and that they should be willing to develop new skills in order to cope with change.   Employees now expect companies to treat them as individuals with a valuable contribution to make to the business, to allow them to carry more responsibility, to offer rewarding career paths and comprehensive training schemes in the technology and in the business, and to allow them greater flexibility in structuring their individual work schedules.

Traditionally, the relationship between companies and their employees has been one based on nineteenth-century concepts of paternalism, of control, and of following rigid rules.   Companies originally planned to exploit IT to strengthen these traditional concepts by making an underlying assumption that more dependence on information technology would lead to less dependence on people.   However, a growing number of companies are now discovering that the converse is true, and that the deployment of IT itself is a dynamic force involving not only technology but people. By aiming to receive a positive return on its IT investments, a company actually increases its dependence on the quality and commitment of its staff.

A number of additional factors contribute to shifting the focus from the technology back to people.   The current research has found the following dynamic forces exist which will further contribute to moving people back to the centre of a company's priorities:

- There are fewer new applicants applying for jobs. Demographic changes, on a European scale, mean that there will be fewer new entrants to the job market in the future. The Institute of Manpower Studies is predicting that, in the UK alone, graduate numbers will stagnate by the end of the 1990s, while demand for them will rise by 30 per cent. In the past, companies have grown familiar with a recruitment routine that has been geared to rising population levels and where the supply of job applicants has always outstripped demand. The selection procedures for trainees could, therefore, with some justification, be restricted to an annual trawl of colleges and schools, where there had always been fierce competition for available vacancies. Now, however, companies are finding that this competition is diminishing and that they can no longer count on automatically attracting the right applicants and on filling all their vacancies. As a consequence, some companies are looking towards schemes to retain and better utilise their existing staff. It has been found that it is possible to direct IT investments towards both these aims, in the former case by dismantling rigid job structures, and in the latter by freeing limited personnel resources.

- There is greater job mobility. Competition to attract experienced staff means that employees are no longer constrained to staying with one company all their working life. Individuals now have a wider choice and can make career changes more easily - even more so in an integrated single European market. While previously new applicants were expected to have a curriculum vitae showing a solid long-term service with a single firm, it is now increasingly accepted that to have an extended number of relevant job changes is a sign of industry-wide experience and breadth of knowledge.

Companies accepting that some employees will only stay for a limited period of time are increasingly turning towards IT to support these new dynamics by using the technology to organise working environments optimally, so that new staff can minimise their time in coming up to speed.

- Those employed are often highly qualified. The extended set of skills needed to do justice to many jobs has led to an increasingly sophisticated workforce. Before the introduction of technology, demands for well-trained staff were more restricted and individuals were often employed to do repetitive, mundane tasks that did not need a large set of skills. In the current market, however, complex work processes now require an increasingly educated calibre of person to be employed. In return, prospective employees now expect recognition of their qualifications and corporate help to further extend these qualifications. Companies that meet these new expectations direct IT towards providing an effective support system where individuals can exchange new ideas, extend their skills and learn from the experiences of their peers.

- Employees expect comprehensive training programmes. In an industrial age, where manual work was most common, educational processes beyond school age were often considered externally irrelevant and financially unnecessary. In contrast, attitudes in the information age are changing and education is increasingly considered of crucial importance. The problem is that the speed of change in the technology and in market conditions is hard to follow and that old skills, methods and procedures quickly become outdated. The solution must be to regularly update educational programmes and to regard education as a life-long process. However, current educational developments in UK companies have been found inadequate and, as a result, are putting UK firms at a disadvantage when it comes to attracting applicants for jobs.

The Government Training Agency Report for 1989 shows that less than one quarter of employers had an established training plan in 1986/7, and that this figure is well below European competitors. To remain competitive in attracting and retaining key personnel, companies will be forced to adapt to providing relevant educational programmes and training schemes as an integral part of their employment policy.

- Employees expect to work with technology. The current research has found that the majority of businesses, in their current form, could not exist without IT. Previously, access to computers was limited to only a few specialists, as their size and complexity demanded that they were situated mainly in the IT departments. Now, however, computers are much more widely available as technological developments, increasing user friendliness, and a sharp reduction in hardware costs, have led to the introduction of PCs and minis outside the IT departments. As a result, technology has become an indispensable business tool for a wide range of employees. These employees now expect to have regular access to processing power. To retain key employees, companies are therefore under pressure to meet these expectations and to make more technology accessible to more people.

- Working from remote sites has now become possible. Technological developments have opened up opportunities for greater flexibility in work structures and processes, so that it is no longer necessary for all employees to work from the same site, or even to work at the same time, as their colleagues. Previously, in order for a business to function, it was necessary to have its key employees at central sites as operations were also strongly centralised. Now, the difficulties of attracting staff to live and work in cities, and the expense of maintaining all operations at sites where space has been at a premium, are forcing companies to search for alternatives. Some companies succeeding in attracting and retaining quality staff are directing their investments in IT towards facilitating the diversification of different work functions to different locations. This presents companies with the opportunity of recruiting staff from other sections of the community, including those who want to work from home, for example women with families, and the disabled.

In the present study, it has been found that all companies investigated are aware of the growing interdependence between employers and employees, and of the need to put people before technology. It has further been found that a significant proportion of companies are already considering themselves to be people constrained, as competitive pressures are developing to recruit and retain key personnel. The problem that surfaced most acutely was how to put the theory of what was widely understood and recognised into practice. Successful examples of companies meeting the challenge of employees' heightened expectations show a change in the attitudes of management towards their employees, in that managers are abandoning their old role of simply directing work efforts, in favour of a new role of being a facilitator, thus enabling individuals to work more effectively.

3.4   CHANGES IN AVAILABLE TECHNOLOGY

Retrospective studies have shown that changes in available technology are strongly affecting the investment value of a company's IT deployment. The value of hardware/software declines rapidly as more sophisticated products are introduced on to the market and as manufacturers stop supporting old systems. Whenever new software appears that offers substantially better business support, but no longer runs on old installations, these installations become obsolete.

To retain the optimal value of its IT investments, a company must learn to adapt to technological change, and increase its understanding of the forces that direct this change. In general, the speed of technological change demands that systems should, as far as possible, be modular and replaceable. Some companies have started to devise detailed life-cycle projections of all proposed IT initiatives. These not only explicitly include the projected life span of systems, but also plan for how these systems will eventually be phased out when becoming obsolete.

Currently available technology continues to grow in power, capability and flexibility, at decreased costs. The power of hardware is multiplying, the costs of processing power are steadily declining, and peripheral devices are becoming more sophisticated. Distributed networks are increasingly being installed. While software becomes not only more reliable and more portable, it also addresses at the same time more business areas. Finally, the interface between computers and users is being improved by applying ergonomic standards.

In combination, these elements indicate that IT is reaching a new level of maturity. Today's expensive state of the art will become tomorrow's affordable standard equipment. As a result, IT will become more visible in the 1990s, and systems that once only large companies could afford to install and to operate, will become commonplace.

Better hardware, more processing power, smarter software, and new interfaces that are easier to use, are based around the following developments:

- Progress in hardware technology is leading to a state where more and more functions are being directly built into the hardware. This will make future software developments easier and more reliable. Storage capacities are undergoing a revolution with the availability of 4-megabyte memory chips and rewritable optical storage devices. Peripherals like high-resolution graphics displays and inexpensive laser printers are gaining in sophistication. Laptop computers are becoming more usable and more affordable. However, the most significant hardware developments over the next five years will be the rise of desktop PCs and workstations. They will become more powerful and considerably cheaper to buy. Currently installed 'dumb' terminals will be replaced by PCs with their own processing power and local data storage. A trend can be observed that indicates that, by the end of the decade, PCs will be installed on the desks of every company employee, including those of the chairman and managing director.

- Progress in increasing processing power available is occurring at such a rate that every three to four years computers double their cost/performance ratio. A recent report published by the OECD, calculated that, over the last three decades, the cost/performance ratio of processing power has improved consistently at a rate of 25% per annum in nominal terms, almost 30% per annum in real terms. The signs are that this trend will continue.

- Progress in software developments is largely achieved by the successful exploitation of research into structured methods and verification procedures. Software houses, in the past often criticised for producing poor quality, are making well-directed efforts to improve their products, and are increasingly seeking out large-scale feedback from their user community. According to OECD, 1989, software houses and related services are expecting to grow at a rate of 20-30% per year. Leading edge technologies like management information systems, knowledge-based systems, voice recognition systems, and optical character recognition systems are producing their first practical results. A continuous flow of new ideas is emerging for the applications of traditional technologies to business functions that currently rely only marginally on IT.

- Progress in the interface between computers and users is making computers more 'user friendly'. Large-scale research into ergonomics is not only producing practical guidelines of how to structure traditional computer interfaces like keyboards and mice, but is also proposing entirely new ways of how to interact with the computer. As user interfaces are further improving, computers are becoming more accessible to more users.

The net result of these developments suggests a continued dramatic growth in the use of IT. Research data shows that revenues for computer manufacturers continue to increase. The worldwide mainframe computer and peripheral market revenue in 1988 amounted to $43 billion and a growth rate of 7-8% is projected every year for the next five years (MIRC, 1989). In the world-wide PC market, revenues in 1988 were $17 billion, corresponding to 6.4 million machines (MIRC, 1989). Growth rate projections are even higher, 20% per year for the next five years.

The combination of these technological advances with the shift in traditional cost structures is placing managers in a dilemma when making IT investment decisions. On the one hand, an objective assessment of technological progress is very difficult for non-IT specialists, and focuses attention on management's own lack of technological understanding, and on the other hand, management is wondering when to invest further in IT, because the high prices paid today might look ridiculous in one or two years' time. Taken together, these two factors often result either in handing over control of new IT investment decisions to technical specialists, or in unnecessarily delaying the replacement of old systems.

Both these reactions have to be resisted; the former because the current study has clearly shown some of the difficulties that arise if IT professionals are left in sole charge of new investment decisions, the latter because deferring IT investments on the basis of falling hardware and software costs is fallacious as the overall costs of installing systems, which include organisational change and human costs, do increase.

CHAPTER 4

CONTROLLING IT INVESTMENTS BY INITIATING CHANGE

To control IT investments, not only has a company to adapt rapidly to the challenges that external changes currently in progress bring about, but it also has to actively initiate change itself in its general approach to running a business. Introducing large-scale IT into a company shifts the way an organisation, and the people in it, work. Moreover, IT changes the nature of work itself. The current study has identified some of the powerful effects that IT deployment can have on both human and organisational issues. It can be observed that while introducing IT magnifies existing conflicts, shortcomings and inadequacies in current work practices, it also affects the deep-rooted nature of traditional work patterns. Particularly, a new emphasis is being placed on effective working relationships that often results in allocating more responsibilities to more individuals. Successive redefinitions of traditional functions and boundaries follow, together with a shift in the distribution of internal political power and a change in the shape of organisational reporting structures. The net effect of these developments is a set of potentially damaging forces which, if left uncontrolled, might well annihilate any economic advantages gained through introducing the technology in the first place. Few companies can afford to leave these developments to chance or to the slow but steady introduction and evolution of the technology itself - they have to be anticipated, managed and controlled.

The following changes have been observed when large-scale IT is introduced into a company:

- New patterns of work emerge. While IT makes it possible to save time by cutting out a variety of time-consuming but mundane tasks, it exposes individuals at all levels to an increased amount of available business information. In many companies this has shifted the focus of their employees' habits and work patterns from simply executing routine tasks, first to understanding the broader implications of these tasks, then to learning about and experimenting with alternative approaches, and finally to taking on a more active role when tasks are initially defined.

- New team formation and working relationships are introduced. IT enables communication between individual members of a team to be drastically enhanced. While in the current study 38% of managers reported that IT has led to a marked improvement in the communication with staff, a further 36% of managers successfully use IT to enhance the quality of communication with other managers. Multi-functional and multi-linguistic team formation has been observed in a number of companies. It is now more often the case than it was a few years ago that teams can function effectively even if the individual members are based in different locations.

- New definitions of traditional functions and boundaries become necessary. IT offers the potential to overcome the traditional splits between different functions which were previously strictly demarcated as a result of the vertical nature of work processes. For many companies this has led to major organisational change as new task allocations within current business units occur.

- New allocations of responsibilities enforce themselves. Evolution of the technology itself enables individuals to experiment with innovative applications of the technology to extend the scope of their current tasks. Some of these innovative applications will always be successful. This results in the innovators' opportunity to extend their sphere of influence and to increase their ability to carry additional responsibility.

- New distributions of internal political power can be observed. Many traditional managers of the 'old school' are still baffled by the technology and do not appreciate that IT is an immensely powerful tool. Introducing IT into the business results in increasing the dependency of the business on IT. Inevitably, managers who succeed in understanding and controlling the technology gain a greater influence in the control of the business itself.

- New organisational reporting structures are being introduced. IT threatens the role of middle management by offering a dramatic increase in the quality of communication between senior and line managers by cutting out redundant intermediary levels. This offers the opportunity to tighten the link between guidance from policy makers and feedback from the operational levels.

Where a company neglects to control IT investments and does not initiate a comprehensive and planned programme of organisational change, change will nevertheless occur but will seem to take on a logic of its own. Without the will and capacity to actively direct this change, case studies show that the impact of large-scale IT will result in altering the political balance of power within a company. This will shift the control from the traditional 'overt' structure to an inherent 'covert' structure (Hirschheim, 1985) where those who have the greatest knowledge about IT or who wish to resist the introduction of IT, can successfully manipulate the issues so that the political forces of the company undermine the intentions of senior managers. If insufficient resources are allocated to addressing the fears and forces that trigger such reactions, mistrust increases, individuals are alienated, there is confusion over responsibilities, dissatisfaction and low morale develop, and waste results.

While few companies participating in the current study can point to a complete all-round programme to anticipate and block unwelcome change and loss of control resulting from the introduction of large-scale IT, examples of good practice do exist and have been investigated in this study. They suggest that to be successful with IT, a company must create a cultural background that stimulates effective corporate use of the technology, must develop a relationship based on trust with employees that encourages innovative exploitation of the technology at all levels, must educate almost everyone within the organisation on the increasing value of information and the evolving nature of information processing systems, and, last but not least, must actively encourage reorientation of some middle managerial functions.

Creating a proactive corporate culture

- recognise people and talent as a company's most valuable assets
- create a climate of trust where everyone feels involved
- nourish a positive set of attitudinal characteristics towards quality, value and customer service
- create a culture where initiatives with IT can flourish
- secure the necessary political and bureaucratic support to plan and implement IT strategically
- eliminate cultural resistance to change

Encouraging risk taking and individual responsibility

- project a supportive attitude towards taking risks
- allow people to take on increased responsibility
- tear down the barriers to flexible job transformations
- encourage individual growth and role expansion
- develop a programme for continuous re-skilling
- provide more accurate value and reward systems

Company

Raising information and IT awareness

- make people aware of the value of information
- train staff at all levels to recognise the potential of IT
- shift the emphasis from doing to thinking
- close the gap between business executives and IT professionals
- encourage participation in seminars and conferences
- forge links with independent external research centres

Redesigning the shape of an organisation

- encourage horizontal rather than vertical management of the business
- decentralise yet control from the centre
- flatten reporting structures
- expose more surface to the environment
- build fluid teams rather than bureaucratic pyramids
- redefine the role of middle management

Figure 4.1 Controlling IT investments by initiating change.

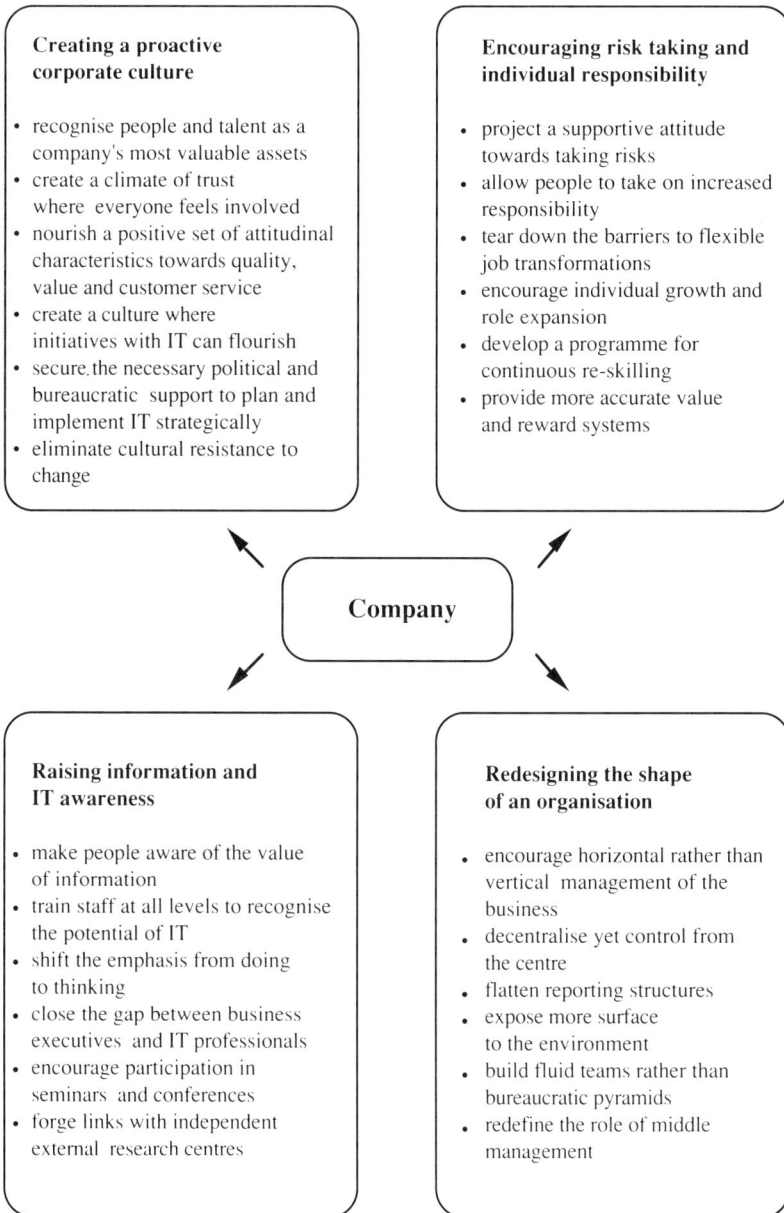

Initiating a programme of active change has become a necessary prerequisite to controlling IT investments. Figure 4.1 illustrates some of the essential ingredients that were found to be needed. In particular, a proactive corporate culture must to be created where continuous development and change become normal practice. Risk taking and individual responsibility have to be encouraged by building new relationships based on trust. Information and IT awareness must be raised so that everyone is aware of the value of shared information. Finally, the overall shape of an organisation has to be redesigned by exposing more surface to its external environment.

All organisational action is largely constrained by deep-rooted habits of how the environment is perceived and of how relationships between top, middle and line management are structured. In order to initiate an effective and comprehensive programme of change that actively involves people at all levels, strong guidance from senior management is required. Deep-rooted habits do not change easily and pockets of resistance are found in all organisations where individuals fear change. Education, discussion, and identification of genuine concerns, help to diffuse these fears. It must be stressed that numerous case studies in this research have revealed that unless a company learns to deal effectively with these issues, the impact of IT on the human and organisational dimensions will be unexpected and uncontrolled.

4.1 CREATING A PROACTIVE CORPORATE CULTURE

The gradual implementation of IT systems throughout an organisation foreshadows a shift in cultural attitudes of the individuals directly exposed to the new technology. This can result in different cultural assumptions between different pockets within an organisation, thereby effectively destroying the common corporate culture. Case studies show that where senior managers recognise these developments, they are able to counteract a split in the corporate culture by closely monitoring the impact of IT on the corporate style. Cultural impediments towards desired change are then removed by isolating attitudinal problems, and a proactive cultural climate is created that supports and furthers the imaginative use of the new technology.

The culture of a company is linked to a number of important functional relationships whose resolutions will determine the overall approach towards IT investments and will therefore exert a direct influence on the return on that investment:

- The quality of a company's internal working relationships between white collar and blue collar employees, between top, middle and line management, and between users and IT professionals.

- The quality of a company's external business relationships between employees and a company's customers and suppliers, and between individual business units and specific market segments.

- The perceived equilibrium between risk taking and risk averseness, between acting on initiatives and reacting to pressure, and between assuming and avoiding responsibilities.

- The relative flexibility of the bureaucratic infrastructure and of local power domains to support cross-divisional and cross-functional projects and to work as a corporate whole.

- The projected self-image, as expressed in the balance between upholding tradition and striving for modernisation, between allowing divisional dispersion and strengthening centralised control, and between welcoming change and resisting change.

The relative success with which a company resolves these issues with respect to the introduction of IT strongly determines the degree to which it will be in a position to draw out everyone's commitment to succeed with the new technology. The internal dynamics of most companies, however, determine that any deviation from the status quo, particularly the attempt to change deep-rooted habits and assumptions in corporate culture, are often resisted. Corporate inertia demands therefore that a well-directed and positive effort is made to facilitate the desired change. A successful return on IT investment depends on how well a company succeeds in getting everyone involved. Wherever anxiety, cynicism and unwillingness to change are present, an effort has to be made to train, to educate and to open up a creative dialogue. If management succeeds in inspiring and nourishing a cultural climate that stimulates new ideas and that enables the company to transform itself into a sustainable innovative enterprise, it forges a valuable key to unlocking the latent business potential always present in a turbulent environment of change and to directing IT investment towards sustaining continued innovation in that environment.

To create a proactive corporate culture conducive to optimising a company's investment in IT, the following examples of good practice have been observed:

- People and talent have been recognised as a company's valuable assets. Companies able to retain key people and to draw out their commitment to the firm's long-term success are forming genuine partnerships and a shared vision between management at all levels, and between all those involved in planning, developing and using IT. In particular, the views of employees are taken more seriously by actively seeking out early user participation in technology-induced job changes. Similarly, talent, wherever recognised, is acknowledged, drawn out, developed and rewarded.

- A climate of harmony and trust has been created. Successful companies are shifting the emphasis from controlling their employees' schedule and physical presence to controlling results. By initiating and sustaining an extended set of effective dialogues that clearly spells out both tasks and expectations, the conditions are being created where employees can increasingly carry their own responsibility over work practices. Strong and effective team building can help to provide a support system where nobody feels left out. A corporate projection of a positive interest in the welfare and development of employees at all levels helps to develop a sense of mutual respect and trust.

- A positive set of attitudinal characteristics towards quality, value and customer service has been nourished. As competition intensifies and as customers become more assertive, some companies are making a strong effort to stop pleasing themselves and to start pleasing their customers. To create the kind of corporate attitudes that lead to a customer centred approach to conducting business, top management is becoming increasingly involved in initiating and leading a comprehensive programme of education aimed at all levels in the company about the value of quality and customer service.

- A culture where successful entrepreneurial initiatives with IT can flourish with great success has been created. To succeed in a business environment that is undergoing rapid change, some companies are actively striving towards encouraging individual initiatives and innovations - particularly in the field of applying existing technology to new tasks. By harnessing people's commitment to unlocking the potential of IT and by putting an effective mechanism into place where ideas can bubble up from users to decision makers, the conditions are being developed where companies can sustain the drive to innovate and to secure a constant flow of new ideas.

- The necessary political and bureaucratic support to plan and to implement IT strategically has been secured. Systems imposed upon an unwilling bureaucracy are difficult to control. To gain the necessary political and bureaucratic support, key individuals influential at the level of local decision making are regularly being consulted and kept up to date on central IT decision making. Bottlenecks in the bureaucracy of implementing cross-divisional IT projects have been removed. Companies report that even within divisions, existing bureaucratic procedures have been simplified by reducing the number of bureaucratic layers between the shop floor and top management. This in turn has enabled their employees to cut through excessive red tape and to speed up change.

- Cultural resistance to change has been eliminated. To create a climate where people are motivated and willing to change, some companies are actively encouraging the learning of new skills, of personal growth and of job transformation. In particular, the traditional role of middle management, which is most threatened by IT deployment, is being transformed to provide a new value-added function. Most importantly, some companies are succeeding in creating a company-wide commitment where everyone involved in the planning, development and use of IT has a personal stake in its success and is therefore willing to accept and welcome a dynamic and changing working situation.

The key attributes of a proactive corporate culture are team and cross-functional thinking throughout the company, a sense of participation and a commitment to success. By overcoming initial corporate inertia and initial resistance to introducing a new set of cultural attitudes, the subsequent need for change, the identification of further change and the process of change itself becomes part of a company's culture.

Facilitating these changes in corporate culture requires more than broad motherhood statements and wishful thinking. Companies that have achieved a good degree of corporate harmony and unity of purpose, while experiencing dramatic organisational change, have placed great emphasis on the benefits of creating excellent internal public relations. Not only does this provide a mechanism for highlighting successful IT projects and individual key contributions, it also provides a medium for discussion which can assist in diffusing potential areas of conflict.

A corporate culture where future changes in market environments, in available technologies and in work practices can be readily absorbed benefits a company both internally and externally. Internally, new developments can be tackled on a united front and management is perceived to be acting not in a dictating role but in a facilitating role. This shifts the emphasis in people's perception of their work commitments from putting in time and going through the motions of work practice, to producing effective results. Externally, new developments in the market environment are welcomed rather than feared and employees at all levels are motivated to search for new business opportunities and to propose ways of adding value to products and services.

4.2 ENCOURAGING RISK TAKING AND INDIVIDUAL RESPONSIBILITY

The degree to which a market, and a company within that market, applies IT to shift the emphasis of competition from volume and price towards introducing personalised quality services and customised products, directly affects the expectations imposed on every manager of what he or she should contribute to a company's success. While traditionally work directions were determined exclusively top down, with middle management in the role of relaying information from the top to line managers and back up again, a turbulent market environment demands a more active approach, more informality, and more individual initiatives at every level.

Success in creating the right conditions for innovative use of IT and in motivating staff to search for new market-led initiatives depends on corporate attitudes towards risk taking and individual responsibility. Some companies are dismantling the traditional barriers preventing key employees from taking calculated risks and are allowing people to assume more responsibility. However, the devolution of responsibility needs to be linked to a strong corporate control structure. In an information-based organisation, showing a relatively flat but strongly integrated management structure, better self discipline from the first-level line manager all the way to top management is required. By introducing a positive set of corporate attitudes towards self discipline, individual responsibility and risk taking, key individuals at all levels are enabled to take on more decisions within their sphere of influence and to carry their own responsibility over these decisions. This places a company in a position where optimal advantage of business opportunities can be taken quickly and effectively.

Case studies of good practice have shown that some companies are changing the rules of traditional work practices and are engaged in various programmes incorporating some of the following elements:

- A supportive attitude towards taking risks is being projected. Most companies are willing to apply already installed technologies to new business opportunities, particularly if little cost and effort is involved, but only a few are willing to venture into new territories and to take risks. Some that do are actively encouraging experimentation at all levels while at the same time providing an effective centralised support function to help individual managers to recognise and judge the risks involved when planning new initiatives. The provision of an effective support system for risk taking has been made possible by introducing a corporate mechanism to monitor and analyse IT initiatives that fail, both within the company and within other organisations. While the lessons learnt are collected centrally, the emphasis is placed on sharing and distributing that information throughout the company. Initiatives by individual managers are then further supported by deregulating some of the decision-making processes so that key individuals have more freedom to act in accordance with their own business judgements. By increasing a company's ability to identify and analyse risks, new investments in IT do not so much resemble an act of faith but more an act of gambling where the odds are known.

- People are allowed to take on increased responsibility. Some companies are preparing their staff to assume more responsibilities, both over IT investments and over non IT based initiatives, by rotating key employees among several jobs to gain a better insight into the business and by cutting through layers of authorisation and justification procedures to speed up the development of new ideas. However, it is pointed out that allowing individuals to carry more responsibility must be accompanied by a tighter structure to control the distribution of that responsibility. In particular, the development of user-driven IT implementations, although desirable in many ways, can result in a three-way split between the perceived responsibilities of top management, line management and IT management with respect to implementation duties and data ownership. Split responsibilities, if uncontrolled, can lead to confusion of who is responsible for the timeliness and accuracy of data and to the danger that information is not collected and distributed effectively. It is now realised that responsibility over data ownership, rather than responsibility over the technology, is a key issue when deploying IT systems and that a positive effort needs to be made to control the distribution of that responsibility at every level.

- Barriers to flexible job structures have been torn down. While the deployment of IT can yield efficiency and effectiveness benefits in performing a particular job, often that job itself will change as a result. Some companies have found that operating in a sophisticated environment supported by IT enables individual business units to cover an extended set of activities and to perform functions that were handled before by other units or other departments. This presents an opportunity to streamline a company, to cut waste and to free additional resources. Examples of good practice have shown that it is possible to take hold of this opportunity by reassessing work allocations, by redesigning the functions of individual jobs, and by encouraging redeployment within the company.

- Individual growth and role expansion are being encouraged. IT often presents an opportunity for individuals to develop their own talents, both by learning more about the business through better access to business information and by learning new skills based on the application of the technology. In a market environment where conditions continuously change and where new opportunities keep presenting themselves, some people increasingly seek to apply their new abilities and to actively develop their own careers. For instance, when secretaries or administrative assistants assume responsibilities for collecting and manipulating key data, they develop a skill in database management. A company can no longer assume that talented employees will be satisfied to remain in the same position if it does not provide an opportunity for personal development and promotion. The major obstacle to individual growth and role expansion is a rigid bureaucratic organisation that expects employees to continue the job they were originally assigned to do. Companies committed to upgrading and broadening the skill in their workforce are actively encouraging individual growth by designing a comprehensive career path for selected individuals, supported by a programme of accelerated learning about the business and the technology.

- A programme for continuous re-skilling has been developed. IT keeps changing the nature of work by introducing increasingly sophisticated equipment into the working environment and by continuously expanding the set of business functions that employees are expected to perform. Individuals are often unable to follow these developments or to do justice to the constant stream of new demands without considerable training and support. While most companies re-skill their workforce when drastic job alterations are imminent, some companies have developed a new attitude towards education and regard skill development not as a mere one-off event but as a lifelong process. This new attitude is then reinforced by a continuous educational programme where individuals are encouraged to join for short courses on a regular basis.

- More accurate value and reward systems are being provided. As IT continues to blur the boundaries between jobs that were traditionally distinct, old reward systems based on job titles become difficult to retain. Furthermore, some employees embrace the multitude of opportunities offered in the current climate to develop their skills and are eager to take on new responsibilities. Others are resistant to participate in change. Traditional reward systems based on seniority therefore no longer accurately reflect the value of an individual's contribution to the success of the business. To provide people with a basis for motivation and self-development, some companies have introduced invigorating reward and recognition schemes based on linking rewards and recognitions to abilities and to results. In particular, an effort is made to reward individual initiatives and innovations that result in increased efficiency or in enhanced effectiveness for the company and to share with key employees the profits resulting from job transformation and change.

The key attributes of encouraging risk taking and individual responsibility are the projection of a genuine interest by a company's managers in the welfare of their staff, a corporate infrastructure that effectively supports the self-development of motivated individuals, a centralised function to support risk awareness and to back up risk evaluation, and a corporate climate of trust where people are free to experiment.

The development of a strong central control of the IT resource allows for the effective devolution of responsibility, so that individual involvement is maximised, risk taking is encouraged within strict controls, and opportunities are developed and exploited, to the benefit of securing the long-term success of the company.

4.3   RAISING INFORMATION AND IT AWARENESS

While IT can be effectively directed to automate traditional tasks and to support decision making, its strongest potential lies in facilitating the exchange of information. However, as numerous case studies have shown, the exchange of larger quantities of information does not necessarily result in individual managers being better informed. An educational programme is therefore needed to guide and control information exchange and to better realise, in business terms, the potential of a company's IT investment. Not only must staff learn how to use information and IT, but how to use it best.

There is currently a lack of clarity about what constitutes an effective educational programme within companies. In many organisations, it has been found that the essential components of educational schemes are often substituted by courses providing only short-term skills training.

Education is not exclusively about technical issues. Education should encompass the broader aspects of what a company stands for, its management objectives and how IT is already harnessed to achieve business targets in other divisions. A broad educational programme must be slanted towards a management angle rather than be restricted to the teaching of technological complexities. This can help to generate a new set of attitudes about the relationship between people and the technology with which they work. New corporate values will emerge leading to a better appreciation of information and the technology that makes manipulation of that information possible. More fundamentally, such a programme can initiate new ways of thinking about problems and offer new tools for solving them.

Specific training how to operate IT equipment is not exclusively about technical issues either. The individual ability and the skill to effectively access information networks and to speedily extract from the system salient data is increasingly becoming a major basis for allocating and reallocating individual responsibility, influence and political power. The majority of managers interviewed in the current study expressed the concern that they were not optimally using all IT facilities available, because they lacked sufficient technical know-how. Managers who neglect technical skill development and training increasingly face the prospect of losing control over information flows and, consequently, diminishing their own corporate influence and political status.

Research at the Kobler Unit, 1987, has identified a positive correlation between companies assessed to be 'highly successful' in their respective market environments and the level of awareness shown within these companies of the business potential of IT. While market leaders might not invest excessively in IT, it was shown that they are better informed about the value of information and the potential of IT to realise that value. Further research indicated that these companies have initiated a comprehensive educational programme designed to reach almost everyone in their organisation. The common philosophy in such programmes is that the development of people has to keep pace with the development of the technology or the two become disjointed with the result that corporate efforts are split into two competing camps, led on the one side by IT professionals continuously trying to introduce more technology and on the other side by business executives continuously resisting any change of the status quo.

Some of the facets of successful educational efforts, amalgamated from examples of good practice, are given below:

- People have been made more aware of the value of information. Technological progress is the single most important factor heralding the coming 'information era'. Competition in the information age increasingly depends not only on the production of traditional products and services, but also on the quality of a company's market intelligence and the effective communication of that intelligence between key personnel to identify new products, services and additional market niches. Companies realising that a new attitude towards information handling needs to be introduced are engaging in efforts to educate people about the value of information and are encouraging a thirst for information. The aim of such efforts is to make the challenge of exploiting the full potential of information a natural ingredient of the managerial practice for every manager in the company.

- Staff at all levels have been trained to recognise the business potential of IT. The current study has established that 64% of companies report that 'there is room for improvement' in the processes that exist for sharing in-house knowledge about IT and its business application. While state of the art technical developments should be left to specialists to monitor and evaluate, an increasing number of employees feel the need to understand the latent business potential of already established technologies. Companies that recognise this need have introduced training schemes specifically oriented towards the management perspective rather than towards the technical understanding of recently installed systems. By educating staff on the business potential of IT, a company increases its chances of effectively motivating and guiding people to continuously search for innovative ways in which to apply current technology to the best advantage.

• The emphasis has been shifted from doing to thinking. The danger of working with IT is that a company often concentrates its efforts on increasing the volume and speed of information exchange rather than on the process of effectively utilising that information. It has been found that the deployment of information technology needs to go hand in hand with a new set of attitudes where the users make a transition from mere information handling - from collecting, storing and distributing information - to thinking about, assimilating and using that information to generate business advantage. Companies realising that information is only of value when it results in better understanding, are educating their staff to increasingly shift the distribution of their efforts from working efficiently to thinking about the effectiveness of their work.

• The gap between business executives and IT professionals has been narrowed. Acceleration in the pace of business change takes place concurrently with acceleration in the pace of technology innovation. As a result there is the danger of a widening information gap between business executives and IT professionals unless a company's efforts to educate are specifically centred around closing that gap. Companies experience that goodwill and commitment themselves are not sufficient. Effective bridges need to be built between IT management and business management, bridges that result in better understanding and in uniting the aspirations of all parties concerned towards a common goal. Some companies expect their systems implementers to work in an ivory tower and isolate DP specialists geographically and socially from the rest of the organisation. However, in an environment of isolation, it is difficult to exchange ideas. A general trend can be observed that this problem is now more widely recognised, and that an effort is made to actively encourage a higher degree of informal interaction between systems professionals and business professionals by moving IT departments back into main offices.

- Participation in external seminars and conferences is encouraged. The current research has found that while companies are often well informed about the amounts of money competitors spend on IT, they are less aware of their competitors' actual application of the technology to support the business. Active participation in seminars and conferences allows managers to raise that awareness, to share experiences and to exchange new ideas. In the current study, only a small majority of companies, 56%, are encouraging key personnel to participate regularly on such occasions, but it is expected that, as progress accelerates, it will be increasingly hard for a company to operate in isolation and to disregard new developments happening elsewhere.

- Links between the company and external research centres have been forged. Independent research centres can offer an analysis of new technologies, of new application areas, and of new techniques to identify and control IT investments and broader organisational change. This provides opportunities for a company to learn from others. Awareness of these areas ensures that a company avoids expensive mistakes when introducing new initiatives and provides it with a solid basis from which to assess risks. In the current sample, while 60% of companies have regular contact with external research centres, there was full agreement by *all* companies that these links can be potentially very helpful and less expensive to maintain than initiating far-reaching internal research programmes.

Further benefits from raising information and IT awareness by an educational process also follow. There is a greater enthusiasm from senior executives for projects that meet agreed investment criteria, whether these projects be the introduction of corporate or of divisional systems. The IT department becomes more appreciated as a service centre rather than a cost centre, and as employees generally become more aware of the business potential of systems already installed, a better utilisation of these systems follows. However, the greatest benefit from implementing an educational programme based around these examples of good practice is a better corporate readiness to meet the challenges of the coming information age.

4.4   REDESIGNING THE SHAPE OF AN ORGANISATION

The advent of the information age permanently alters the internal shape of organisations, as vertical command structures increasingly yield to horizontal information exchange. While large-scale deployment of IT provides the potential for creating new and tighter organisational interdependencies, the new ability of management at all levels to access powerful new information flows through IT forces companies to realise that potential and to engage in major organisational restructuring in order to gain the maximum benefit from their IT investment. In the long run, continuous changes in market dynamics will not necessarily favour the best equipped organisation, but will favour the best organised.

Traditionally, the shape of an organisation has been based around a highly structured vertical hierarchy where communication paths were strongest along the vertical axes but weak or even non-existent along any horizontal axes. In one company interviewed, where horizontal communication was very poor, the central office was comprised of a number of departmental heads who in turn guided their department by filtering business objectives down the divisional hierarchies. Each division then acted like a separate company within the organisation with divisional work proceeding rather independently from work in all the other divisions. While horizontal communication paths within the top levels existed, these did not filter down the organisation. As a result, middle and line managers in different departments did not exchange information with each other and did not share valuable experiences of how best to cope in an environment of change. In fact, the organisational rigidity often reinforced the separation of divisions and produced unproductive divisional competition for corporate resources.

As the transition from the industrial era towards the information era accelerates, this shape of an organisation is increasingly inappropriate. Data processing functions which had been viewed as central begin to look peripheral. Information exchange, which had been peripheral, begins to appear central. Companies have reported that out-dated, multi-layered and vertical organisational structures give rise to conflicts between the existing structural rigidity and the need to introduce new cross-functional service centres. A rigid hierarchy limits understanding by individual units of the corporate whole and often leads to the erection of functional barriers, to duplication of efforts and resources, to individuals protecting their part of the organisation and shifting the blame whenever mistakes occur, to unnecessary bureaucracy, and to the general attitude that information is the property of the division that holds it, and not the resource of the organisation as a whole. As a result, corporate rigidity becomes a serious constraint to the effective utilisation of the new technology, and is often the reason why the productivity gains achieved by IT regularly fall short of both expectations and technical potential.

In contrast, a further case study illustrates that when desired change in the organisational structure was initiated by top management, the company was able to benefit from the reduction in the tiers of the hierarchy by cutting overheads and by shortening top management's response to environmental changes reported by line management.

The emerging paradigm of a typical company in the information age, as assembled from examples of current good practice, shows that organisations will be more complex and more sophisticated. The structure of future organisations will be based on a new fluidity that facilitates networks rather than hierarchical bureaucracies. Interest in rules and procedures will be replaced by an interest in the identification of tasks and in working in teams. Reactive production processes geared to defending a hold on current market niches will be replaced by an active enterprise culture searching for advantage.

Companies in tune with current market dynamics have already initiated the following changes:

- A horizontal rather than a vertical management structure for the business has been introduced. As the pressures to coordinate activities such as quality control, introduction of better services and imaginative use of the new technology across the whole of the organisation increase, some companies are changing traditional management practices by breaking down the barriers that enforce an almost exclusively vertical management structure and have started to manage key issues horizontally at all levels. While previously access to information depended on a person's position within the structure, IT is now employed to enable managers, particularly middle and line managers, to overcome traditional departmental boundaries. It is now feasible to establish and maintain horizontal communication lines between individual business functions of a similar nature, or between business units operating in a similar field, even if these functions and units are located in different divisions.

- Operations have been decentralised but are still controlled from the centre. In an environment of change, there is a general need to move closer to the front-line of the business, so that change can be recognised at an early stage and a company can adapt more rapidly to new demands. As a result, a trend can be observed where successful companies are replacing a highly centralised corporate management structure with a more decentralised, fragmented, regional structure based on profit centre management and management by objectives. To integrate, guide and control regional efforts with respect to the overall corporate business strategy, companies are educating their staff to develop a new set of attitudes based around commitment and responsibility. To minimise the problems of duplicating efforts and of learning the same lessons repeatedly in each region, decentralisation is supported up by the introduction of excellent communication links between similar territories across the company. To minimise the danger of losing central control, IT is employed to facilitate data exchange between each region and the centre. Paradoxically, as devolution increases, a corresponding need to centrally control and monitor developments and to promulgate the flow of ideas throughout the system also increases.

- Current reporting structures have been flattened. By exploiting the potential of IT to strengthen communications between all levels, companies are now concentrating on utilising human resources more fully by changing jobs originally designed to supervise, to jobs that add new value. While the three basic levels of management, i.e. directional management at the top to set objectives, functional management in the middle to allocate resources, and operational management at the bottom to identify and implement tasks, still exist, the degree of control and authorisation levels previously needed within these management levels has been cut. The typical successful company now shows fewer levels in its management structure between top and line management. However, according to a report by the Institute of Administrative Management and the Confederation of British Industry in 1987, management-to-staff ratios of 1:2.4 showed that in general the UK is still far behind the USA, where the better companies are achieving ratios of 1:4.8. The report concludes that in some companies up to 50% of staff costs are accounted for by the management structure and argues that this is insupportably high.

- More organisational 'surface' is being exposed to the environment. In the attempt to create an organisation that is perceived by customers as 'customer friendly', companies now concentrate on making their internal functions and processes more transparent to their clients. The aim is to remove the red tape preventing customers from speedy access to their records and to additional services required, even if these are spread across a variety of departments. Whereas before, a customer was forced to deal with several departments for different enquiries and services, IT is increasingly enabling a company to serve all customers' needs from a single business unit. This requires a new cross-functional approach that will increase the interdependency between different functions. The internal structure of a company is then organised not according to traditional functions and processes, but primarily according to products and customers.

• Fluid teams rather than bureaucratic pyramids are being built. Companies are still learning how to operate optimally in an increasingly international market environment that includes more diverse cultural groups. The problem is that while current market dynamics demand an extension of the scale of a company's operations, they demand at the same time a greater range of products and more individualised services. Some companies meet these challenges by abandoning traditional bureaucratic pyramids and by establishing new extended multi-functional and multi-cultural teams. Such teams often reside in several locations incorporating, possibly, an international dimension. In the effort to orient business conduct around effective teams rather than around pyramid structures, companies are now increasingly looking for individuals who are good team participants, rather than for individuals with an extended range of skills but who can only work in isolation.

• The role of middle management is being redefined. Applying IT to a company's information resource is changing that resource from a traditionally passive archive to an active and effective means of distributing information. As a result, middle management's role as active propagator of information between top and bottom is being reduced. The current study has found that in some companies middle management is resisting change and is dragging out the effective deployment of IT because of fear that its role will be threatened. Managers can be extremely effective in resisting changes that they see as being personally disadvantageous. The problem is that while some middle managers' jobs are value added, others are more administrative and therefore more feasible to automate. If this is indeed the case, a restructuring within the company is needed to cut out unnecessary overheads and to add value to all middle managerial positions.

The net effect of changing the shape of an organisation according to newly identified needs is an increase in the core activities - traditionally around 20% of a company's efforts - that directly support key business objectives and customer needs; a decrease in support activities - traditionally around 60% - that enable the core activity to be performed but add no value; and a reduction in discretionary activities - traditionally around 20% - that result from doing things wrong the first time round. Further advantages of redesigning organisational reporting structures are the development of new skills as individuals work in teams where members share an extended set of abilities, and a more effective utilisation of resources, particularly of already installed information technology.

CHAPTER 5

CONTROLLING IT INVESTMENTS THROUGH A CORPORATE INFORMATION STRATEGY

The results of this study suggest the need for a fundamental reassessment of the way in which a company should operate in an age where information flow and information management increasingly assume the principal concerns of management. Case studies have shown that senior executives of successful companies emphasise the importance of information as a vital corporate resource, a resource that has equal status with finance, raw material, manpower, and other major assets. There is a growing consensus among managers that information will be *the* key commodity in the coming 'information era', and that the ability to compete successfully in an increasingly information-driven economy will primarily depend on management's ability to effectively control, manipulate, and distribute this commodity across all levels of an organisation.

The current research has shown that most companies enter the information age with a lack of accessible information. Typically, information needs have been neglected or have been analysed on a simple piecemeal basis, thereby losing any strategic coordination and control. As a result, two main problems arise: either a company suffers from information starvation where not enough shared data is available to allow individual divisions and senior management to operate effectively, or a company suffers from information overload where too much data is available, but salient information is so hidden that it is simply not accessible.

In the first case, vital corporate information such as data relating to customer buying patterns, or data identifying general market opportunities, is collected but is kept isolated in individual pockets throughout the organisation, with the result that it is inaccessible outside the immediate working environment. This ultimately leads to a loss of business for the company as a whole. Managers in different divisions, often dealing with the very same customers or with very similar market situations, are not aware that corporate information exists which can be potentially effective when aiming to pinpoint and seize business opportunities.

An example of how information starvation can lead to corporate waste is the company which conducted a divisional feasibility study of desk top publishing systems. A particular requirement was to link such a system to an existing company-wide UNIX network. After careful analysis of the latest products, involving repeated discussions with suppliers, consultants and software houses, it was decided that an Apple system, originally favoured for its ease of use and low price, but found wanting in terms of power and compatibility, could run effectively under the corporate network. With only a little adaptation it would indeed fulfil all the corporate needs. However, as current funding had already been fully allocated, implementation of this project was postponed. Unfortunately, the results of the completed study were not made available to other divisions, and senior management subsequently discovered that corporate resources were repeatedly wasted as other divisions planning the introduction of DTP systems were not aware of this work, and became engaged in expensive consultancy contracts to solve the very same problems.

In the second case, 70% of managers complained that they were swamped with too much information without an effective filtering process to highlight salient data. Information overload is now recognised as a problem that has taken on epidemic proportions.

In most cases, information overload is a direct consequence of having introduced IT on an *ad hoc* basis, without analysing the exact information needs of those managers to whom the information is to be distributed. Companies agree that if the exchange of information is not rigidly structured and individually tailored to different levels of management, it becomes an expensive mass of data, slowing down the progress of a company and causing confusion.

As an example, in one particular company, it is current practice for divisional managers to prepare and exchange monthly reports stating the progress of all running projects. As these reports are written on departmental word processors, each report is an update of and elaboration on the last edition, and consequently is more voluminous. At the time of the study, a typical report consisted of around 200 pages. Each divisional manager, receiving 10 reports from the other 10 divisions each month, is indeed hard-pressed to find out where progress had been made, and whether any lessons learnt elsewhere might be helpful in achieving his own goals. As a result, the reports are not read and the exercise is a waste of valuable time and a loss of opportunity to share vital experience.

In order to avoid the problems of generating too little or too much corporate information, a comprehensive and coordinated corporate information strategy is required. Such a strategy should spell out a common information infrastructure, a set of general directions, the reason for the strategic direction and its major consequences. It is the only means of guaranteeing that top level strategic decision making can be based on the right kind and right amount of salient information.

The objective of a corporate information strategy is to ensure that the quality of horizontal cross-divisional communication is increased, that effective cross-functional linkages between overlapping activities exist, and that vertical information flows between different management levels reflect practical information needs. In particular, an information strategy aims to:

- identify a hierarchical structure of critical information needs using a suitable form of abstraction to avoid information overload, and to address these needs precisely at each level of management

- provide the means for managers to move easily between multiple levels of information abstraction

- introduce guidelines on the manner in which critical information is to be collected, where it should reside, and who is responsible for keeping it current

- decide which data is proprietary and sensitive, and what steps are to be taken to ensure security against loss and theft

- assess both formal and informal structures currently in place for exchanging critical information

- improve on current structures by introducing a thoroughly integrated common information infrastructure for sharing critical information across the organisation. Such an infrastructure has to reflect the way in which the business currently operates, but has to be flexible enough to readily adapt to future changes in business and technology.

As changes in market conditions accelerate, the need for an information strategy becomes more prominent. Without clearly defined processes for updating which information is critical to competitive success, companies are finding that they have vast resources committed to keeping out-of-date material accessible. A formalised information strategy enables flexibility to be built in, so that the needs of the company and of managers are always the main focus. Having better access to information allows managers to do their jobs better.

The formulation of an information strategy does not include prescribing any technical implementations. Indeed, not all information needs are best fulfilled by technical means. There is a need for informal channels of communication where 'soft' data can be freely circulated. Non IT based information exchange like company specific 'grapevines', social meetings, or regular gatherings outside company premises do exist and have to be acknowledged as an integral part of an organisation's information infrastructure. Attempting to formalise these processes more rigidly does, however, lead to wasted resources and increased distrust among employees. The essential function of an information strategy is to facilitate the flow and exchange of business relevant information. If this is done successfully, informal information channels will work to a company's advantage, will strengthen morale, and will speed up the learning experience across divisions.

5.1   THE FRAMEWORK

The Kobler Unit Information Strategy Framework, given in figure 5.1, is based on the extensive research of both successful and unsuccessful management practice. In the current study, no single company investigated was found to have a fully developed and comprehensive strategy to deal with information exchange and information needs. As a result, information management remains largely patchy and is generally tackled on a piecemeal basis. Extensive discussions with company managers have, however, indicated the need for guidelines to construct a comprehensive information strategy framework. Such a framework has been assembled from pockets of identified good practice in a broad range of companies. Its main components, as identified by the Kobler Unit, are the dynamic unification of business mission, competitor modelling, market performance indicators, customer feedback, operational needs, and IT opportunities into a consistent and relevant set of management goals. Once such a set of goals has been agreed upon, it can then be analysed in terms of general information needs and concrete information requirements as a basis for generating a corporate information strategy.

```
┌──────────────────┐                      ┌──────────────────┐
│ Business Mission │ ───▶           ◀───  │ Customer Feedback│
└──────────────────┘                      └──────────────────┘

                        ┌──────────────┐
┌──────────────────┐    │     Set      │   ┌──────────────────┐
│   Competitor     │ ──▶│     Of       │◀──│ Operational Needs│
│   Modelling      │    │  Management  │   └──────────────────┘
└──────────────────┘    │    Goals     │
                        └──────────────┘
┌──────────────────┐          │           ┌──────────────────┐
│Market Performance│ ──▶      │      ◀──── │  IT Opportunities│
│Indicators        │          ▼            └──────────────────┘
└──────────────────┘
                        ┌──────────────────┐
                        │General Information│
                        │Needs              │
                        └──────────────────┘
                                 │
                                 ▼
                        ┌──────────────────┐
                        │Concrete Information│
                        │Requirements        │
                        └──────────────────┘
                                 │
                                 ▼
                        ┌──────────────────┐
                        │Information Strategy│
                        └──────────────────┘
```

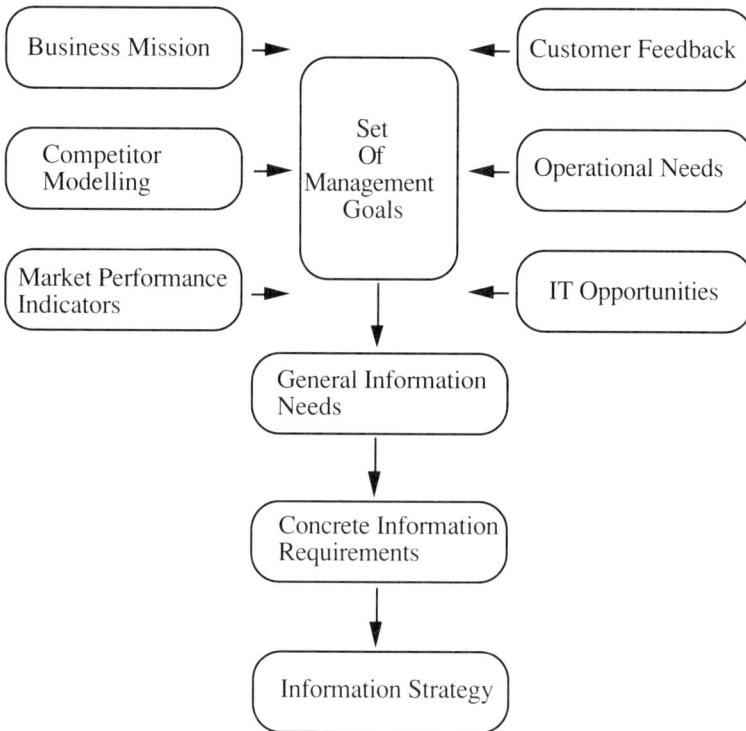

Figure 5.1 The Kobler Unit Information Strategy Framework.

125

By 'business mission' we understand a short and concise written statement containing the vision of the company leaders as it relates to the aspired business direction and market impact of the company (product range, degree of diversification, degree of risk averseness, attempted market share, attempted company growth, aspired public image, geographical spread, etc.). It is a statement from the top that is filtered down the corporate hierarchy to guide all planning processes. To be effective, the company mission should be publicised, easy to understand, and inspire efforts on all levels.

By 'competitor modelling' we understand the introduction of a procedure to accumulate and disseminate information about competitors' activities, in particular about activities relating to the use of IT. The current research has shown that only 29% of companies are aware of competitors' use of IT to open up business opportunities. As a company's capacity to block, match and anticipate IT-related initiatives launched by competitors becomes increasingly vital for business survival, a stronger awareness is needed about the potential impact of such initiatives. Detailed case studies suggest that companies acquiring a thorough knowledge of their competitors' IT investments, types of IT applications, and the benefits that have resulted, are put in a stronger competitive position. They are also prevented from making rash investment decisions as a reaction to rumours about the benefits obtained by a competitor.

By 'market performance indicators' we understand a set of diagnostic benchmarks about the relationship between productivity, costs and overheads. Such indicators are based on the performance of a peer group outside the company, and are used to compare a company's business characteristics with comparable organisations. Typically, they contain data on the horizontal and vertical integration of management, on organisational complexity, and ratios on costs/overheads and management/labour distribution. By incorporating information about relevant market performance indicators into strategic planning, a company can ensure that strategies are well in tune with the realities of current market situations. If a company finds its own performance for specific operational processes below par when compared to the performance of the overall market sector, the business units concerned have to be isolated and a fundamental re-evaluation of current strategic plans in these areas is needed *before* proceeding to analyse detailed information flows. To deduce and automate information flows which do not contribute towards overall business success is not only a self-defeating exercise but will result in investing in the wrong information infrastructure which, once implemented, might be difficult to change afterwards. As has been well documented, e.g. by Strassmann, 1985, the application of information technology to business objectives will have a magnifying effect upon the strengths and weaknesses of current practice. Only if a manager's success in reaching specific business objectives in terms of 'par' is high to start with, does it make sense to decide what the concrete information flow structure should be in order to provide optimal support.

By 'customer feedback' we understand the identification of a customer's changing needs and expectations. This information should be actively sought for specific customer profiles, and then fed back into a centralised corporate database. Such a database can then form a cornerstone of product development and quality control, both of products, and of customer services offered.

By 'operational needs' we understand the needs and activities at the level of line management which have to be undertaken to achieve the set of corporate goals. For instance, a general management goal such as 'improve management information for decision making' needs to be broken down into specific objectives that can be clearly identified and understood. It is important to realise that details discovered at operational levels often affect high level corporate goals, and that bottom-up feedback on strategic directions is a necessary ingredient to the formulation of a realistic information strategy.

By 'IT opportunities' we understand an exploitation of the business opportunities which IT offers. Case studies indicate that information technology often has an opportunistic component which is easily missed in the planning process, but which can subsequently be realised. Existing systems, installed for a particular and well-specified purpose, can often be extended with minimal effort and investment in order to offer additional competitive and strategic advantages. To exploit these opportunities, strategic planners need to be made aware of innovative ideas and of ways of using existing systems more effectively. Such information can be provided by establishing an effective information channel for updates on the accelerating changes of the technology itself. This channel can then be accessed in a bottom-up manner by line managers, by users, by the DP department, or by outside consultants.

By a 'set of management goals' we understand an internally consistent set of corporate aims, directions, and efforts of senior, middle and line managers across all levels of a company. This set has to be relevant in respect of the realities of external market forces. Obtaining such a set will be the first milestone towards creating a corporate information strategy.

By 'general information needs' we understand an outline of those information needs that must be fulfilled to ensure that the set of management goals can be realised. As these goals change over time in accord with the dynamics of the market, the information needs themselves will correspondingly change.

By 'concrete information requirements' we understand the actual specification of the general information needs identified. To translate information needs into specific requirements, the focus has to be shifted from abstract conceptual models to concrete and detailed designs.

As an example of how these concepts interact, a hypothetical case of an automobile association can be used. The company might aspire to fulfil the mission 'to become the most effective British automobile association in terms of offering customers the fastest, most reliable, and most extensive service available'. To fulfil the company mission, a manager might aim to reach every stranded vehicle in a shorter time than the competition, and to increase the number of repairs which can be done on the spot above that of the competitors. Feedback from customers might reveal that more effort is required to offer the best general motoring support available in terms of cheaper insurance cover, better road maps, and more accurate travel guides. To formulate these objectives in terms of management goals, specific competitor information and the overall performance of the entire market sector have then to be taken into account. For example, by comparing cost/benefit ratios per rescue team, or ROI between different kinds of IT investments and company performance with identified market norms, a company can gain useful indicators of where future efforts are likely to be most effective. Further assistance in formulating management goals explicitly is provided by feedback from below, when these objectives are broken down into the detailed operational needs. For instance, to increase the number of repairs on the spot, the level of staff training might be recognised as being crucial. Training needs themselves must therefore be incorporated in the set of management goals. Finally, opportunities provided by newly available technologies, for example portable computers able to run an expert diagnosing system for staff in the field, can then be exploited as and when they arise, as a support to the overall management aim of providing a better quality service and thereby gaining a competitive advantage.

To generate an information strategy that is based on an explicit set of consistent and relevant management goals, *all* these elements of the proposed information strategy framework have to be taken into account. The current research has shown that management goals and business strategies are often formulated with some of these elements missing at the planning stage, with the result, acknowledged by companies, that subsequent IT installations stem from the wrong perception of management's true needs.

5.2   THE PLANNING TOOLS

While an information strategy framework identifies the basic components of an information strategy, a planning methodology is needed to formalise these components explicitly and to merge them into a coherent whole. To do justice to the complexity of internal and external forces involved, neither a top-down nor a bottom-up approach to planning suffices. Instead, a participatory approach is needed, combining the top level view of senior managers with bottom line perceptions and feedback from users and line managers.

An exclusive concept of linear top-down strategic planning is unrealistic on several accounts. Firstly, it was noted that it is impractical to prescribe that in order to be successful, a company must first devise a full-blown top level business strategy and then devise an IT strategy to align with it. The results show that in practice, top level business strategies generally do not exist, or if they are written down at all, they are in the form of lengthy documents which are usually out of date by the time they reach the desks of key managers. Hence there is often no solid point of reference with which to align information technology. Secondly, it was noted that a linear top-down methodology often produces a strategy that is in danger of being externally irrelevant. Such a danger is brought about by a planning process that is strongly biased towards an out of date view of current strategic opportunities, and is designed to preserve the status quo and to prevent strategic efforts from taking external changes into account. Thirdly, it was noted that as little room is left for iterative feedback from below, the final strategy is often incomplete as it does not address the more subtle changes in market demands. In particular, if a company operates in a turbulent environment, any planning process which neglects feedback from below is in danger of failing to identify current needs. Fourthly, it was noted that even if the attempt is made to control all external forces and to plan for all contingencies, the costs of developing such detailed plans are unacceptably high, and the time delay in implementation is too great for companies actively involved in competition for market share.

An exclusive concept of bottom-up planning is equally unrealistic, as such a method lacks strategic direction, vision, and leadership from above. Whereas line managers should be encouraged to seize opportunities wherever they occur, and to generate new initiatives, these individual efforts have to be combined into a strategy that is internally consistent. If internal consistency is lost, individual managers in the organisation will work towards different and often contradictory goals. Furthermore, a bottom-up planning approach frequently means that systems organisers or IT professionals are in charge with the result that often good solutions are found, but for wrongly identified problems.

The current research has shown that successful managers, always under intense pressure to boost short-term profitability and to secure long-term shareholder value, increasingly alternate in time between fulfilling long-term top level business aims as stated in the company's overall mission, and reacting to immediate threats and opportunities in order to decide their overall strategic approach in a chosen market sector.

What is needed is a participatory approach to strategic planning which recognises that top-down guidance and bottom-up iterative feedback must be combined into a unified whole. Top-down contributions will include the generation of a mission statement, the modelling of competitors, and the awareness of market performance indicators. Bottom-up contributions will include feedback on the changing needs and expectations of customers, logistics of crucial details discovered when management goals are further broken down, and identification of potential IT opportunities as and when they arise. Such an approach necessitates a structured dialectic process with both an individual and group focus. While knowledge elicitation techniques will be essential for generating individual points of views, group techniques and team work will be needed for testing individual perceptions and combining them into a consistent whole. This can only be achieved by the active and continuous participation of key personnel selected from all levels and involving senior, middle, and line management.

The first milestone towards a corporate information strategy is to generate a set of management goals. As management goals provide the foundation of an information strategy, it is vital to focus on corporate goals which are of strategic value to the company. Such an approach guarantees that subsequently implemented systems are directed towards high impact areas, and that they address issues critical for the business.

5.3   CRITICAL SUCCESS FACTORS

Critical success factors (CSFs) are those few key requirements which must be fulfilled to ensure success for a manager or a company. CSFs, if consistently realised, are the foundation on which future strategic directions can safely be planned. If the CSFs are not achieved, they will become *the* major obstacles to further corporate progress and will ultimately result in a loss of business. As such, CSFs are key areas of broader organisational concerns, requiring every manager's special attention and a team effort that must span all levels of a company.

Critical success factors can be broken down into detailed management tasks and general management information needs. To take the automobile association example again, if a critical success factor is to reach every stranded vehicle within 30 minutes of receiving a distress call, the detailed management task might be to station and man service teams in an appropriately spaced geographical grid and to dynamically adjust this grid as teams become engaged or for any reason are not operating to full capacity. The general management information needs to accomplish this task will include having continuous access to the latest information on the current state of readiness of each team, and information about relevant past team performances to allow as good a projection as possible of the most likely developments needing particular management attention.

From the point of view of generating a corporate information strategy, a breakdown of CSFs into critical tasks to be performed is a very useful and practical method of making explicit vital information flows throughout all levels of a company. Case studies repeatedly show that CSFs can only be achieved optimally if a conscious effort is made to streamline and direct information resources and activities to the specific goals of managing the underlying critical tasks and processes effectively.

As a methodology in its own right for making management goals explicit, for translating these goals into detailed tasks, and for identifying the general information needs to accomplish the tasks, CSFs were first proposed by Rockart (1979). However, while the original application of the methodology has been aimed exclusively at eliciting the information needs of Chief Executive Officers, the method can easily be extended to provide a more generic procedure for strategically planning information needs at every level of a company, and horizontally across individual divisions and functions.

An extended method based on CSF, demonstrated by the Kobler Unit, and by others, to have been acceptable to both senior management and line managers, is directed towards three distinct areas:

- to identify the set of top-level corporate goals by management, irrespective of the presence or absence of an explicit business strategy.

- to isolate the detailed tasks, processes, and resources needed to optimally achieve the identified set of goals. This will also provide iterative feedback on the set of goals.

- to derive a high-level specification of the general information needs required to enable the detailed activities to be performed effectively.

The method can be repeated in a hierarchical fashion to identify the information needs of senior, middle, and line management. A detailed procedure for applying the method in a practical way as a first step towards generating a corporate information strategy is given by the following sequential steps:

- sponsorship of a CSF project by a senior manager responsible for corporate information management

- briefing of a skilled CSF analyst on the market situation in which the company operates, on its general mission and internal reporting structures

- engaging in a series of structured dialogues between the analyst and key managers from all levels of the company

- eliciting the personal CSFs of each manager by conducting individual one-two hour interviews

- consistently referencing the personal CSFs with one another at each level of responsibility

- refining the collection of personal CSFs obtained by group discussions and by a first breakdown of the CSFs into detailed tasks and processes

- synthesising the refined personal CSFs into a collective and consistent set of organisational CSFs for senior, middle, and line management

- identifying general information needs to support an optimal accomplishment of the tasks specified.

The wider benefits of applying the method to the definition of an organisational information strategy are numerous. In particular, a CSF method:

- expresses the information needs of salient business aims

regardless of whether an explicit business strategy has been defined or not

- enables the board and senior management to adopt a unified planning approach for achieving business goals

- emphasises learning by increasing managers' appreciation of the critical importance of sharing vital corporate information

- generates involvement across the company, with the result that managers at all levels increasingly work towards goals they have defined themselves

- fills the well-known communication gap between senior management and IT professionals

- is easy to understand and use, and does not require a heavy commitment of organisational resources

- helps to understand and accelerate corporate reorganisational efforts for adapting to and for initiating change

- has a positive effect on the development of group dynamics and team building with the result that political problems diminish.

By following an extended CSF methodology, a consistent and relevant model of general information needs can be derived. This model then needs to be translated into concrete information requirements by using standard techniques such as as object-oriented approaches, functional decompositions, application generators, rapid prototyping, or CASE tools.

5.4   CONCRETE REQUIREMENTS

To succeed in thoroughly identifying concrete information requirements, the point of view of the information receiver, and not of the information provider, has to be taken into account. This demands simultaneous attention to three related issues:

• the content of the information to be provided

• the form in which the information will be presented

• the procedures involved in accessing the information.

The content of the information to be provided needs to be based on the general information needs, as established at each layer of the corporate hierarchy by, for example, the CSF methodology. A successful identification of concrete information requirements is demonstrated by the case study of a particular company, assisted by the Kobler Unit, that resulted in the following requirements:

• Improved sharing of market information between divisions. The need was expressed for circulating more information about market share and about market conditions. All the information was paperbound and hard to obtain, and facilities were needed to allow managers to be able to plot market information graphically against last year and against the rest of the market.

• Improved sharing of customer information at all levels. As several divisions wanted to run telephone enquiry services for customers, the following information was needed to be instantly accessible: current projects, involving each customer, a cross-reference to similar projects implemented elsewhere, a complete list of projects implemented so far for each customer, business units and people involved in both current and past projects and the detailed accounts for each project. Also, a need was expressed for collecting and sharing information about the customers' own projections of where new areas of business opportunity might arise in future years.

- Improved sharing of technical information. This was to prevent each department 'reinventing the wheel' when engaging in feasibility studies. Information was required in the form of practical feedback about any application developed or tested elsewhere within the company, a general evaluation of what is good and why, and a contact person within the company who is already familiar with a particular product.

- Improved sharing of project information, in particular, making easily accessible a list of current projects, the state of progress and manpower on each project, a projection of further resources needed, and various contact names for finding out more about each project.

- Improved sharing of skills and training information. As the business of the company was people constrained, the skills of personnel were an important asset that had to be effectively managed and developed.

Besides specifying the content of information, the form in which the information will be presented has to be given serious consideration. When analysing *what* information a manager needs, it is essential to take into account *how* this information will be displayed. The medium for representing information cannot be divorced from the information itself. For instance, if the information is to be accessed via a display unit, the actual presentation of the information on the screen can facilitate or obstruct a manager's perception of what data is currently important. The analyst has to find out from the user, possibly with the help of rapid prototyping, what particular form of presentation is most useful for highlighting salient data. Decisions have to be made regarding, for instance, the use of graphical representations of data, the use of colour and sound, how to gain the user's attention when critical data has changed, how much information is optimal to display on a single screen, how to move from one information source to the next, and how to break down high-level data into more detailed figures.

The analyst might well find that he cannot fulfil a particular information need if the technology employed is unsuitable for presenting this information in a form that is genuinely helpful for the user. For example, a manager might insist on working with a single graph showing multilayered histograms, each in a different colour, representing financial data such as costs, turnover, and profit. If the terminals installed have no colours or only a poor graphical interface, they will be unsuitable for satisfying the requirements and the graph will have to be produced using another medium, such as a traditional wall chart. It makes no sense to specify an information strategy that subsequently cannot be implemented or which will be implemented in a cut-down version which is entirely unhelpful to the user. To do so is not only a waste of money, time and energy, but results in confusion and general user hostility towards further change.

Of equal importance to information content and form are the procedures involved in accessing the information. Again, these procedures are an integral part of an information strategy and have to be specified *before* an information infrastructure is set into place, as particular configurations for accessing procedures will influence and to some extent determine detailed information requirements. If useful information is potentially accessible but awkward to get at, it loses much of its appeal and potential value. Indeed, such a situation is similar to the problem of information overload where salient information is somewhere in the system but is inaccessible for all practical purposes.

In practice, the user will often have to be presented with several options where information depth and speed of access are traded one against another. If, for example, the analysis of past market performances for different sets of data varies considerably in processor power required and therefore in processing time, the user will have to choose a particular installation configuration that is both practical and useful. Similarly, if the user needs access to a consistent set of marketing data from his office terminal, from his home PC, and from his laptop field computer, he might be forced to trade access to some potentially useful data against his requirements for overall consistency.

The form in which information is presented and the procedures involved in accessing information are as important as the actual content of the information. Unfortunately, most companies, when analysing information needs, are not aware that the kind of information managers need, how they want that information presented, and what procedures they are willing to follow to gain access to that information, are all intricately interwoven with one another.

Once individual information needs have been analysed, a corporate information strategy can be formulated. The success of the strategy will depend primarily on how well the horizontal integration of individual requirements is tackled, and on how well vertical abstraction can be achieved to gain a suitable view of details at any level .

Horizontally integrating individual data into a transparent but coherent information structure is a basic requirement of every information strategy and not just an implementation detail. Information systems have to be integrated with one another to the point where data will have to be input only once, and where it is possible to easily switch from one database or application to another. For example, if a manager plans a new project for a customer he might first search a technical database for the latest product information, and then decide what kind of people he will need to implement the project by accessing an in-house skills database. Having found the necessary skills, he will want to know the general background of the employees with these skills using a personnel database, access a customer database to find out whether any of them have already worked on past projects with the customer, and then use a project database to establish what these employees are currently working on and when they will be available. The ease of use by which the manager can switch from one database to another will ultimately determine the success or failure of structuring and computerising a process that was once performed using hard copies, the telephone, and personal meetings with various in-house business units.

Vertical abstraction leading to a suitable form of information detail can be achieved by a strict hierarchy of key information needs for the central coordination of the company, for the top management of each department, and for managers of specific business units. Much thought and effort has to be put into generating a structured, multi-layered information flow where a variety of applications can stem from the same database and where different depths of information can be extracted from the same document.

Identifying corporate information flows and managing information distribution effectively are key tasks for today's companies. Success in these tasks will give managers at every level in the corporate hierarchy access to both horizontal and vertical information flows with the exact degree of detail and abstraction needed. Lack of information definition and lack of effective distribution of information will result either in information overload or in information starvation.

Only a corporate information strategy can guarantee success. Such a strategy has to be initiated, reviewed, and managed by a senior manager responsible for corporate information management. The Kobler Unit proposes that to design and control an information strategy, the position of a chief information officer or information executive should be created in companies with the specific tasks of looking at the business from an information angle, of identifying opportunities for improving information resources throughout the company, and of educating management to view information as a key commodity that must be coordinated and managed.

CHAPTER 6

CONTROLLING IT INVESTMENTS THROUGH A CORPORATE IT STRATEGY

While the information strategy delineates those information needs that are critical for a company's success, an IT strategy specifies how some of these needs are to be fulfilled. It is important to realise that the main thrust of an IT strategy is to plan the implementation of the information strategy, and that an IT strategy can therefore only be specified if an information strategy has first been put into place. If implementation is not preceded by a comprehensive IT strategy, as has been found in 66% of cases in the current study, a company will subsequently experience a strongly increased number of IT-related difficulties. This suggests that the relation between strategic planning and business success is a major hallmark distinguishing successful from less successful companies.

The value of an IT strategy has to be measured primarily in terms of its relevance to business needs, and only secondly in terms of its technical sophistication. Systems efficient at performing inappropriate tasks do not contribute towards the organisation's goals. The organisational objectives have to drive the technology, not the other way around. Once information needs have been structured down to the level of concrete information requirements and implementations of these requirements, fundamental changes in information flows are hard to accommodate and will first necessitate a major review of a company's information strategy. It

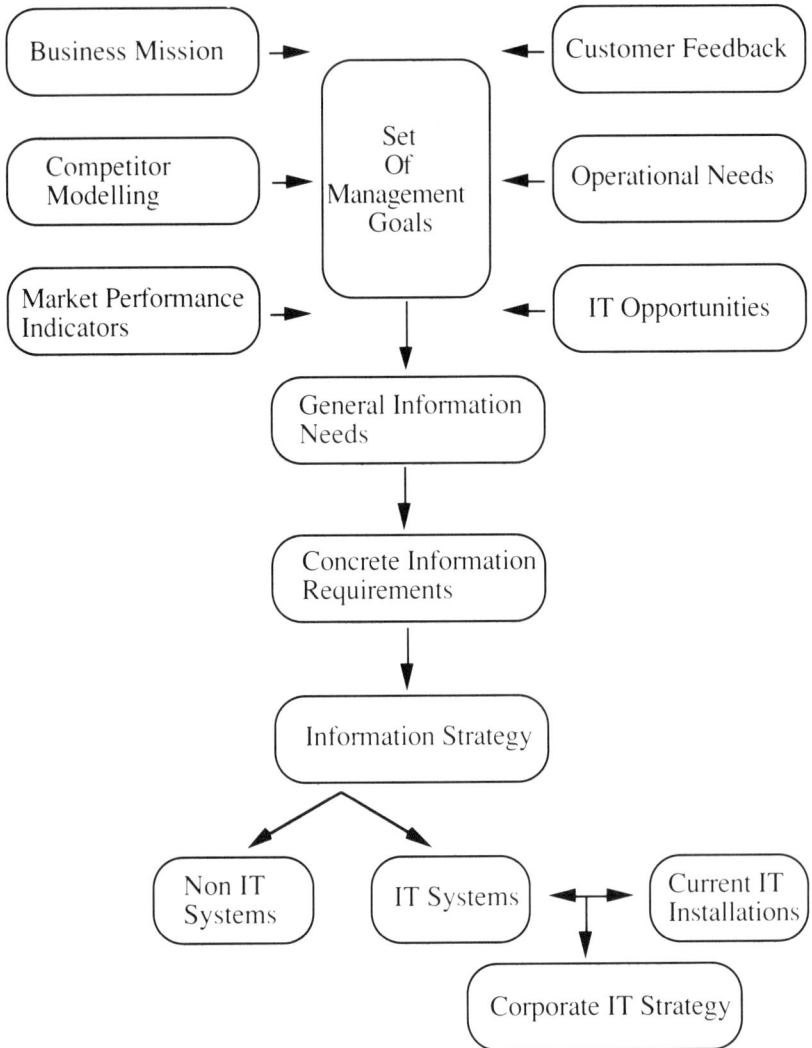

Figure 6.1 The Kobler Unit Information and IT Strategy Framework.

is therefore important that *all* IT investments are based on a thorough information flow analysis which ensures that the investment is explicitly aligned with salient information needs and business goals.

As indicated in figure 6.1, the first step towards formulating an IT strategy framework is to generate a corporate information strategy. This strategy is then translated into concrete information systems - both IT and non IT based. An IT strategy is then devised by integrating the planning of further IT based information systems with IT installations and facilities currently in place.

The objectives of a corporate IT strategy are to plan the implementations of IT systems over a medium to long-term horizon and to give guidelines on all IT related matters. Such a plan has to be written down and made available to all managers in the form of a strategic document prescribing and coordinating all activities relating to IT investments. According to the current research, while a minority of 34% already have a defined IT strategy, no single company investigated is entirely satisfied that its written strategy addresses all the relevant issues. Extensive discussions with company managers have, however, indicated that the following composite plan, assembled from pockets of identified good practice in a range of companies, incorporates the essential elements for successful planning and controlling IT investments:

- Evaluation issues:
  The business benefits of proposed IT systems have to be evaluated by an appropriate evaluation technique and according to corporate standards (see Chapter 1.2).

- Organisational issues:
  Introducing IT brings about change in the organisational culture, in current work practices, in reporting structures and in the traditional distribution of power and responsibility. The organisational consequences of that change have to be explicitly addressed and planned for (see Chapter 4).

- Cost issues:
  The true costs of the proposed implementations have to be calculated, taking account of hardware, software, installation efforts, changes in the physical environment, running costs, maintenance costs, security costs, networking costs, training costs, and broader organisational costs (see appendix C).

- Policy issues:
  The responsibilities of IT management, user and IT departments have to be set and guidelines given on the use of outside resources, acceptable vendors, and contract negotiations (see Chapter 1.4) .

- Control issues
  Ownership, responsibility and review structures of the IT strategy have to be made explicit and a corporate framework for project management put into place (see Chapter 6.3).

- Technical issues:
  A corporate systems architecture has to be specified together with the protocols of data communication, interfaces to divisional systems, and general implementation standards (see Chapter 1.5).

- Systems issues:
  The current systems portfolio and indications of the projected lifetime of individual major systems currently in place has to be given (see Chapter 7).

- Implementation issues:
  The implementation plan indicating major milestones in the migration path from the current IT portfolio to the desired scenario in 3 to 5 years has to be made explicit (see Chapter 6.1).

- People issues
  The level of in-house resources in manpower needed to install, monitor, and service IT installations has to be determined, and training needs of users have to be identified (see Chapter 4.3).

The current research has shown that the majority, 66% of companies, do not devise an IT strategy. Furthermore, it has been found that those companies that do generate a formalised and explicit IT strategy, often address only a small proportion of these central issues. The style and type of many plans shown to the Kobler Unit as IT strategy documents have ranged from one-page wish lists to massively complex technical documents, without business focus. This suggests a general uncertainty about what an IT strategy should contain, about what level in the organisation the strategy should be aimed at, and about who is held responsible for generating the strategy.

In the present study it was often found that the IT strategy was being formulated by the technology division, with little understanding of the broader business issues involved. The current study showed that while more than a third of companies interviewed were concerned that those who determine IT plans had a poor understanding of the business, 25% of managers complained that the board was not sufficiently interested in participating in the generation of an IT strategy. The drawback of leaving the planning of the IT strategy entirely to the IT department is that while objectives dealing with technical requirements for further enhancing current systems are often clearly spelled out, issues concerning the true costs of the proposed installations, projected wider organisational changes, expected business benefits, general company policies, control issues, and people management, are left unspecified. These issues cannot be dealt with satisfactorily by IT professionals, or by any one department alone. While the function of the IT department is to act as a technical implementation resource centre, it is only marginally involved in the development and planning of business issues. It therefore becomes inevitable that if the formulation of the IT strategy is left to systems designers, the technology will become the main focus and will dictate business conduct rather than the other way around.

Unless a corporate initiative is taken to integrate technology development within a business context so that *all* the issues involved in generating a comprehensive IT strategy can be explicitly addressed *before* any implementations are planned, the probability that a company will subsequently experience substantial difficulties due to the introduction of the new technology will drastically increase. If companies proceed to introduce IT without an explicit overall plan, systems designers will be fully stretched trying to keep inappropriate systems operational, or will be tempted to continually develop installed systems by changing or taking on additional facilities. The outcome of this type of unstructured approach to IT planning is that projects take on a momentum of their own, and often become increasingly monolithic and unmanageable. This has been shown to have a detrimental effect upon staff morale, and consequently it becomes more difficult to retain and recruit additional personnel.

Although IT is seen as an investment issue by most of the companies taking part in this study, case studies have revealed that there is often a strong and sometimes counter-productive reluctance to free resources to work on an IT strategy and to convince management to address these issues explicitly. This attitude needs to be replaced by a more constructive approach regarding IT as an investment with measurable and positive returns. It must be stressed that the resources allocated and the effort spent in generating a corporate IT strategy are not considered to be overheads, but will actually *save* a company money by ensuring a better return on what is already being spent.

6.1   PLANNING THE IT STRATEGY

A common fallacy is to assume that a company's actual IT implementation has to evolve in technological stages, and that the company has to be put on a computer systems migration path. Systems engineers often propose that stand-alone systems are developed first and that these are subsequently subjected to a number of integration steps leading to larger and larger networks and contributing to increased mutual compatibility. It is then further claimed that only by evolution can communication be extended from an individual unit to a group, to a department, across the whole company, and finally, to bridging the gap between suppliers, the company, and its customers. Whereas such an evolution can indeed be observed in the short but intensive history of IT, it is not a prerequisite for success that each company should replicate each of the steps of this historical progress.

The current research has found that effective management systems do *not* evolve or merely emerge, but are imposed according to a well defined top-down analysis of needs explicitly seeking out the collection and integration of bottom-up feedback. Instead of asking 'what can this system do for us?', what it requires is the question 'how can we use IT to meet our business objectives?' Successful companies have had the experience that to secure both user commitment and the willingness of (middle) management to change, interim solutions belong on the drawing board, and not on the desk of company employees. To gain enthusiasm at all levels, exposure to IT cannot be managed by installing immature systems. There is only one evolutionary path companies of today must follow, and that is to evolve from a first generation piecemeal approach to IT investments into a second generation approach which strategically plans IT investments *before* actual implementations begin.

The bottom line of any IT strategy is to show how IT can best support the medium and long-term business goals of management.

It is therefore necessary to draw up an adequate time frame in which such a strategy is operative. Experience has shown that one- year planning and budgetary cycles are not adequate for the development of the IT portfolio, as both business objectives and implementation complexities often span a more distant horizon. A more realistic time frame for strategic medium to long-term planning is to choose a horizon of three to five years. An IT strategy can best be formulated by first generating a number of different scenarios of how IT can support the role and the impact of the company on the designated market environment within the time frame advocated. These different scenarios can then be rated by senior management as to the extent to which they best support the corporate vision as laid out in the mission statement, while still offering optimal flexibility to adapt dynamically to changing information needs as dictated by evolving market complexities.

Presented with the favoured scenario of where a company would like to be in terms of its IT portfolio over the next three to five years, the obvious challenge is where to start. As no company will start from a 'greenfield site', a thorough understanding of the architecture and the applications currently in place is needed. Current facilities, often either outdated or under-exploited, will have to be evaluated by both users and IT professionals as to their potential for contributing towards the desired portfolio.

The next step is to define a migration path from the present facilities and systems to the facilities and systems required to support the strategic vision. Maintaining the course of development of IT-based systems on this defined migration path becomes of strategic importance, and as such overrides many of the more pragmatic considerations which, because of their less than strategic perspective, would almost certainly have otherwise defined the choice and role of systems support facilities.

Once individual systems planned for development within the horizon specified have been identified, implementation priorities have to be set. In order to maximise all investments - money, time, personnel, and other resources - strategic planners must establish a clear definition of how to determine implementation priorities. It has been found in the current investigation that often insufficient attention is given to defining the priority attached to each project proposed or in hand. Instead of the 'single dimension' priority-setting used in many companies, a 'multiple dimension' priority-setting should therefore be considered. Each proposed project can then be rated on the extent to which it:

- is an infrastructure project essential for allowing further IT developments that promise a high commercial payoff
- contributes to high priority corporate business goals as identified by a CSF analysis
- temporarily disrupts current operational practices, thereby possibly inflicting a short-term loss of business on the company
- requires scarce and valuable resources within and across departments
- is a mandatory requirement.

As annual or more frequent revisions of long-term strategy occur, the migration path taken by the IT function to go from present systems, to those required to support the business three to five years hence, will shift as well. The implications of shifting corporate objectives need to be fed back into the IT planning at a strategic as well as at an operational level, otherwise the investment in IT may be wasted and operational systems may be undermined. However, it was noted that the effects of change in corporate objectives on IT planning can be mitigated by having good data administration, data modelling standards, and system modularity.

6.2   IMPLEMENTING THE IT STRATEGY

The criteria for successful IT implementations are twofold: users have to accept and utilise the system, and the investment has to produce an appropriate return. If a system does not satisfy *both* these requirements, the implementation cannot be declared to be a success.

Given these criteria, the degree of success achieved in practice by companies implementing IT varies considerably. A number of retrospective studies, for instance Romtech, 1989 and *Business Week*, 1989, have found failure rates of 70% and more for computer-based information systems. These figures have been verified by Kobler Unit research, where it was further established that most companies acknowledge the problem and are now more determined to increase the ratio of successful implementations, as the mistakes and the subsequent disruption are proving extremely costly. According to detailed research, carried out by IBM in 1988, a typical problem costing £100 of analysis time can cost up to £10,000 to fix after implementation.

The current study has found four main reasons why systems implementations often fail to be successful:

- the implementation is technically correct but is based on an inadequate analysis of user needs
- the implementation is very sophisticated but is not based on any analysis of true business needs
- the implementation is a short term success but subsequently proves to be too inflexible to further develop as user needs change
- the implementation is technically consistent but does not succeed in capturing *all* of the user needs specified.

The first problem, correct implementation of an inadequate analysis of end user needs, stems from the difficulty of defining the detailed user requirements at the pre-implementation stage. It is a well-known fact that users are unable to specify their exact information needs in a systems vacuum where they simply cannot imagine how the final implementation will affect, change and redefine their current work practices. As pointed out earlier on, it should never be assumed that users can deliver accurate and detailed information systems specifications, as the optimal system will depend not only on the information content but also on the form in which the information will be presented, and on the procedures involved in accessing the information. The lesson to be learnt is that systems implementation and requirements analysis cannot be rigidly separated.

To avoid the dangers of correctly implementing an inadequate specification, end users have to be more involved in the actual implementation process. The present study has shown that only 58% of companies actively seek out user participation. This attitude needs to be changed. Case studies of good practice have shown that if users participate during various key implementation stages and are regularly consulted to provide requirements feedback as implementation proceeds, the resulting systems tend to be more used than technically superior systems developed by a remote agency. To succeed in involving end users, the use of application generators for rapid prototyping is recommended as it greatly facilitates iterations of potential implementations and provides an opportunity for end users to experiment with the system and to adjust their detailed requirements accordingly.

The second problem, implementations which are very sophisticated but are not based on any analysis of true business needs, stems from unresolved political power struggles within a company. This particular set of problems was found to exist in companies where either middle management was threatened by a comprehensive programme for restructuring current practices, or where the IT department had gained too much influence over new IT initiatives. The technology is then introduced for reasons that are totally unrelated to true business needs, as for example wanting to keep pace with technological sophistication, or wanting to deflect attention away from the current problems, e.g. low staff morale and other uncomfortable organisational issues. The lesson to be learnt is that the role and responsibilities of both middle management and IT professionals have to be kept under review and made explicit.

To avoid the danger of introducing IT for political reasons, any disruptive internal tensions and power struggles must be resolved before actual systems are implemented. Case studies show that when IT is introduced for political instead of for solid business reasons, it is usually done by people who have a totally misinformed understanding of the actual content of people's jobs, and of the way in which IT will help or disrupt the work pattern of the organisation. IT is an enabler and should be introduced with the principal aim of facilitating people's work. By introducing IT for any other reason, a company exposes itself to the danger of investing in an expensive toy which has no tangible business return on the investment.

The third problem, implementations proving to be only short-term successes, stems from the difficulty of defining how user requirements will change over time in the light of new ideas and changing market conditions. In the past, the attitude often prevailed that user needs will remain static, that implementation is a one-off process, and that the quality of the implementation should be judged primarily by the speed of its execution. Therefore, only minor emphasis has previously been laid on the importance of the internal structure of the implementation, and on the quality of systems documentation. To fulfil the criterion of speed, systems were written in low level languages incorporating numerous optimisation routines directly in machine code. As a result, the implementation code was often too complex to

understand and subsequently to alter when the need to do so
arose. Case studies have shown that systems analysts often spend
80% of their time in understanding code already written. In the
current study, 75% of companies suffer from the presence of old
systems which cannot be updated within reasonable time scales.
If users want additional functions, it is found that it is often easier
to write a new program and then to link this new program to the
old system. Facilitating electronic data interchange, however, has
proved to be a particularly difficult and time-consuming process.
The majority of companies consistently report that incompatibility
problems between different pieces of hard and software is a
serious constraint in optimising the effectiveness of the
investment. Sometimes the same data often has to be manually
input several times. This makes the corporate IT system slower to
use and less reliable. The lesson to be learnt is that information
needs are never static but evolve over time, and that systems
implementing current requirements need to have the same level of
flexibility built in to keep pace with incremental change.

To avoid the dangers of devising systems which are inflexible and
incapable of being updated when future needs change, different
measures of what constitutes success will have to used. Instead of
judging systems exclusively by power and speed, more emphasis
needs to be placed on the nature of the implementation itself,
particularly on the use of high level structured programming
languages generating code that can be easily understood. Systems
will need to be designed that are modular, so that it becomes
possible to update a single module without disturbing the rest of
the implementation. The quality of systems documentation will
also need to improve to facilitate understanding of the
implementation when subsequent updating becomes necessary.

The fourth problem, i.e. technically consistent implementations
which do not succeed in capturing *all* of the user needs specified,
stems from the difficulty that the finer points of both software (i.e.
environments, operating systems, languages, and application

generators) and hardware itself, are impossible to assess without actually putting the system through its paces. Whereas the current study has shown that 25% of companies are disappointed by the performance of their hardware, a much larger proportion voiced concerns over the quality of current software, particularly if bought off the shelf, as being often rather poor and imposing restrictions on systems design. Ultimately, these restrictions will be felt by the user and will have to be balanced by introducing additional, non IT based information systems. This will result in additional work, dissatisfaction, and slower information access. The lesson to be learnt is that a partial implementation of user requirements is not a correct implementation, and is more associated with failure than with success.

To avoid technical restrictions imposed by hardware and software platforms, a common procedure for evaluating and testing these platforms has to be put into place. The procedure should not be based solely on systems documentations but should, if possible, include investigations into the actual practice and user satisfaction of similar systems currently in use elsewhere. The current study has shown that only 54% of companies contact another firm already using the product/system when evaluating potential installations. There are indicators that this practice is slowly improving as large-scale user groups and collaboration with independent research institutes become more prominent.

Examples of good practice have shown that sophisticated implementation management can avoid these four dangers. Whereas a certain 'chance factor' is associated with having the right implementation experts at the right times at hand, the probability for long-term success is greatly enhanced if a company has a comprehensive management reporting structure in place responsible for IT investments. In terms of implementation management, project teams incorporating not only IT professionals but both users and implementers, have been shown to deliver more acceptable and cost effective results. Such teams are particularly successful if they are chaired by an independent business manager from another section within the company who has a good understanding of the company and can negotiate between all parties concerned.

The implementation team will also be responsible for implementation audits. Communication between users, IT planners, and IT providers improves and the repetition of mistakes is avoided if projects are audited and reviewed regularly. Long term projects should be exposed to audits at least on an annual basis, not only from a continuing relevance and technical point of view, but in order to ascertain whether the priorities attached to projects are still correct, and to review the performance of those involved in the project.

In the current study it has been found that successful companies are using their IT strategy as a framework to guide implementation objectives over time. Trying to implement and control all aspects of IT deployment in one grand exercise simply does not work. Those companies that have established a strategic implementation plan over time, are not only succeeding in reaching their short-term objectives, but are also succeeding in gaining a stronger-long term control of their investments.

6.3   MANAGING THE IT STRATEGY

As the corporate IT investment grows both in size and in importance, the successful management of that investment over time becomes more and more crucial. Most companies have reached a level of IT involvement where IT can no longer be managed as a mere support or service activity, and can no longer be thought of as a specialist activity that can be safely left to the IT department. What is needed is a new attitude of managing IT strategically in close affiliation with other business functions, and to integrate IT into the company's current planning, control, and operations. This cannot be done by simply expanding current spheres of responsibility, but only by a qualitative change in traditional structures of responsibility. As a company's IT involvement will not remain static, it needs a management mechanism ensuring movement through time in a planned way. This helps a company to keep track of good and bad IT experiences, thus enabling it to learn and to transfer success across internal boundaries.

The current research has shown that senior managers of successful companies tend to be better informed about the performance of their IT installations than their counterparts in less successful companies. While the former tend to hold a tight central grip over new developments and, if difficulties arise, provide a central support, the latter are in the habit of authorising new initiatives locally and managing their installations in relative departmental isolation.

To enable strategic management of IT, the Kobler Unit recommends the setting up of a corporate IT planning group (not a committee) led by a senior executive, reporting to and being responsible directly to the Board. It is recommended that this group be staffed by secondees of merit drawn from a variety of individual business divisions. These members should be able to spend at least six to nine months, if not longer, in the group, where this is feasible. The group should further include a small number of full-time representatives from the IT division experienced in corporate planning or quantitative methods.

The responsibilities of the group are to coordinate the development and regular review of both the corporate information strategy and the corporate IT strategy, to supervise the identification and evaluation of new IT initiatives, and to regularly review and comment on the success of installed projects. The group will be responsible for the coordination of all IT investments, ensuring strategic objectives are not thwarted by misdirected expenditure on IT to meet only the short-term needs of a small section of the company, and for interpreting IT and technology developments to the Board.

The existence of this group would further allow for:

- the opportunity for serious study of alternative scenarios for corporate IT developments by individuals highly qualified and highly motivated but temporarily without operational responsibilities

- the opportunity to generate ideas as well as responding to and helping to develop ideas that might originate in other areas

- the opportunity for those who may eventually help lead individual business units to gain a corporate perspective of the business and a better understanding of the constraints and opportunities provided by IT and other support activities

- the opportunity to study competitors' developments with respect to their IT strategies and use of systems, and to search for new high pay-off IT initiatives, possibly outside the present portfolio of corporate activities

- the opportunity to draw attention to and arbitrate between potential conflicts arising from bottom-up initiatives/top-down directives and competing power groups within the organisation

- the opportunity to analyse Board suggestions for development diversification or divestment more objectively and quantitatively

- the opportunity to conduct further research into effective IT management with respect to the IT management structure, the procedures, policies, and methods currently in place.

The resources for establishing such a group would need to come from the corporate purse rather than from individual departments which are always under pressure to increase their own profitability. By using the group to maintain a strong link between the business and the IT department, between the individual divisions and between the board and line management, the planning, implementing, and managing of a company's IT strategy is given a more central role in a company's efforts to regaining control of IT investments.

CHAPTER 7

SUMMARY

While companies are poised to spend more on IT than ever before, a growing number of managers report that they are deeply concerned about the effectiveness of their existing IT investments. The majority of companies now regard IT investments as being a normal capital expenditure from which a positive return is expected, yet 84% of companies are investing in IT without using satisfactory methods to calculate either the true costs, or the true benefits, of that investment. It is now realised that many of the traditionally applied evaluation techniques are inadequate, and that no single generic evaluation procedure can do justice to the variety of business functions supported and made possible by current IT investments. Instead, an eclectic approach, which requires a thorough analysis of the primary objectives of planned systems, and of the inevitable second order human and organisational effects, needs to be taken.

Traditional accountancy procedures for setting IT budgets are found to be too limited, and need to be replaced by budgets that align with the life cycle of IT planning and implementation. The allocation of responsibility for IT to the finance department is increasingly being questioned, as the pervasiveness of IT in most companies has been accompanied by the growth of a powerful information infrastructure, which needs to be actively managed and controlled. To provide the necessary control, some companies now appoint an Information and IT executive with access to the Board.

An IT strategy is needed. While 85% of companies report that IT is becoming an equal partner with other business functions, only 34% of companies introduce IT strategically across the organisation. The results clearly show that companies with an IT strategy in place subsequently encounter less IT-related problems. The evidence suggests that often it is the market itself that will dictate certain types of IT investments for companies operating in particular industries. In order to remove waste and duplication of resources, some industries are considering pooling some resources for infrastructure investments and concentrating on gaining advantage by the individuality of value and quality of products and services offered.

The true business potential of IT can only be realised when IT is directed simultaneously towards streamlining a company's internal efficiency, towards enhancing its external effectiveness, and towards creating new business opportunities. The results presented show that some companies are achieving tangible business benefits by capitalising on the imaginative use of IT to improve the economics of scale and the economics of scope. Many companies, however, still insist that IT must be placed on an evolutionary path, graduating from internal efficiency, to external effectiveness, and only later to opening up new markets. As a consequence, they are placing too strong an emphasis on directing future investments to optimising the internal workings of their organisations, and to automating existing processes, rather than on the imaginative use of new technology to enable new business to be created.

Successful companies are controlling their IT investments by continuously adapting IT to the evolving dynamics of the current business environment. Changes in market conditions, in customer demands, in employee expectations, and in technological progress are reported as the most important new challenges facing management. The indications are that without a close analysis of these factors, companies lose control of their IT investments.

A recurring theme in this study is the observation that the introduction of IT alters the internal dynamics of a company and has a strong impact on human and organisational issues. An analysis of these second order effects shows that to keep control of IT investments, a company has to initiate and endorse a comprehensive programme of further change. This must be directed towards creating a proactive corporate culture, towards encouraging risk taking and individual responsibility, towards raising information and IT awareness, and towards redesigning the shape of an organisation. The role of management itself is thereby changed from a dictating role to a facilitating role, and a new emphasis is placed on building multi-functional teams.

Seventy % of managers complain of information overload or of information starvation. This suggests that a comprehensive information strategy must be formed *before* an IT strategy is put into place. The Kobler Unit Information Strategy Framework identifies the necessary elements that such a strategy must contain, incorporating explicit detailed objectives, and practical guidelines combining top-down and bottom-up planning approaches. A participatory approach is proposed, based on a consistent and relevant set of critical success factors.

An information strategy can then be broken down into a systems or IT strategy. However, the objectives of an IT strategy are not only to present technical directives, but also to give guidelines for *all* IT-related matters, so that there is a well-orchestrated plan along which to control IT investments. Methods used in the costing and evaluation need to be standardised across the organisation; broader organisational change must be assessed; policies need to be continuously improved; control functions relating to data security and data ownership have to be implemented, and training requirements must be addressed. Implementation issues can be supported by steering a company along a migration path leading from current realities to an aspired future scenario, and by the introduction of a multiple dimension priority setting for individual projects. Successful management of the IT strategy over time will then depend on management's ability to resist short-term gains and to aim for long-term success.

APPENDIX A

BACKGROUND TO THIS STUDY

The Kobler Unit is a research centre and IT management consultancy based at Imperial College, University of London. The Unit was founded in 1984 with the particular aim of improving the methods adopted by British Industry for controlling investments in IT, and for assessing the effects of broader human and organisational change, caused by the introduction of the new technology. Under the direction of its first Head, Professor Igor Aleksander, an independent rigorous research programme has been initiated and unbiased information about current good and bad investment practice has been collected with the aim of creating an environment in which no one is slowed down by mistaken IT policies. The Unit also provides a sounding board for new ideas and methodologies and has contributed to specific research carried out by academic partners and industrial researchers in the field. A wide range of companies have consulted it on particular issues of concern, related to their own IT investment. This has led to the Unit being retained by a number of businesses for an in-depth analyses of information needs, for evaluating current investment policies, and for identifying ways in which the return on the investment can be increased.

During the past three years, the Kobler Unit has collected and validated a significant amount of data on best investment practice in IT. This research has been divided into a Phase One and a Phase Two. The results of Phase One have been published in the Report *Does Information Technology Slow You Down?*, which is available from the Unit. This Report has received extensive publicity and was reviewed/mentioned in the following papers:

Financial Times (11.11.87, 3.12.87 and 17.2.88), *Computer News* (19.11.87), *Electrical Review* (25.11.87), *Business Computing and Communication* (November 87, January 88), *Insurance Systems Bulletin* (January 88), *British Institute of Management Journal* (January 88), *South African Financial Mail* (February 88), *Personal Computer World* (March 88), *The Economist* (23.4.88), *Computer Weekly* (10.11.88), *Director* (May 88 and December 88) and *Management Today* (January 89).

Phase Two follows on from this work. The process of gathering information has remained substantially the same for both Phase One and Phase Two. While a confidential questionnaire has provided the framework for gathering factual, quantitative information about current practice, an integral part of the methodology has been to meet the IT decision-makers of each company face to face, in order to elicit relevant information of a more qualitative nature, such as gauging current attitudes, degrees of commitment to IT, and extent of IT awareness. These meetings have also provided the opportunity for more extensive discussions of the main issues raised by the completed questionnaires and for some feedback to be given to the particular companies concerned. In addition to the individual case studies, wide-ranging discussions have taken place with other research organisations, institutes and businesses to broaden the extent of the current study and to ensure that new findings and industrial research are taken account of and are fully acknowledged. Throughout this research the Kobler Unit has been given access to highly confidential material that has provided a privileged view of the internal workings of many of the companies investigated.

The research for Phase One was based on the detailed case studies of 15 companies. Each company's IT involvement was analysed using 40 different factors, covering 15 distinct management areas.

Additionally, the organisational performance of each company was assessed. This concentrated not only on return on capital employed, but also took into consideration a company's profitability history, a peer comparison, staff turnover, customer relations and documented business plans for the medium and long term future. By analysing a company's general business success, independent criteria were established. A formal statistical analysis, based on Spearman's rank correlation, was then performed comparing the general success of acompany with each of the 15 main areas of its IT involvements. In particular, it was assessed whether companies that were leading in their respective market sectors differed significantly in their use of IT from their lagging competitors. Some of the highlights of this phase of the current research are summarized below:

- No correlation was found between the amount of money invested in IT and the general business performance of both leading and lagging companies.

- However, leaders (i.e. market leaders) are actively exploiting their IT investment, whereas laggers tend to show a reactive attitude and allow their work to be driven by the possibilities and limitations of particular IT installations.

- Market leaders employ a solid IT investment policy based on a corporate IT strategy which is aligned to the general business aims of a company - laggers tend to justify new IT investments in terms of cost-cutting or as an act of faith.

- Leaders differ significantly from laggers by exploiting IT for management advantages, especially in the area of communication and decision support.

- Leaders have stronger ties to IT resource centres and show a higher awareness of the potential of IT than laggers.

- Leaders are better informed about the performance of their IT installations than laggers and tend to get a better return on their IT investment.

- Leaders determine the priorities of different IT projects centrally - laggers invest on a piecemeal basis determined by the demands of individual departments.

- Both leaders and laggers report that the most difficult task in getting to grips with the new technology is not technological know-how but how to *manage* their current IT investment successfully over time.

Phase Two is based on the detailed case studies of 34 companies. The investigations focused strongly on the relevant key areas of successful IT investment as identified in Phase One.

In order to establish a company's approach to each of the key areas identified, an interrelated series of questions, some written, others the basis for discussion, were formulated. Using the results of Phase One, each of the questions was directed towards an area where either leaders have been shown to differ significantly from laggers, or where both leaders and laggers experience the greatest difficulties. As a result of defining relevant key areas in Phase One, Phase Two could concentrate on investigating these in more detail and record the difficulties both successful and less successful companies experience, as well as what solutions are most effective.

PARTICIPANTS
Although the names of the specific companies that agreed to take part in Kobler Unit research will not be disclosed, the following information about size, industrial sector and position held by the

person who represented the company's IT involvement, can be made available.

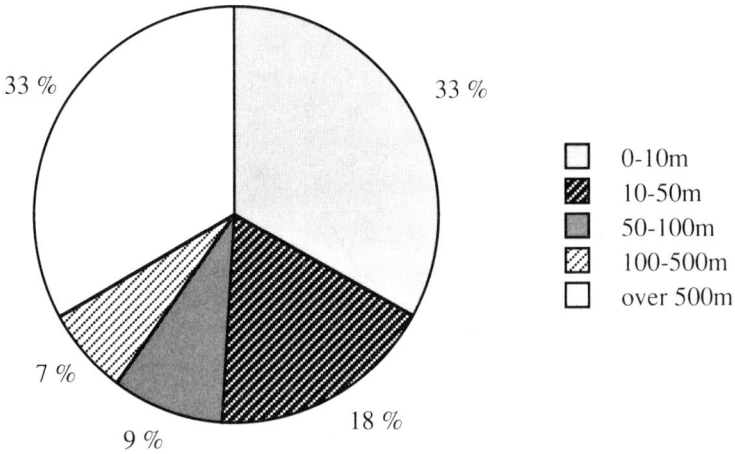

Figure 1 Response according to company size (turnover).

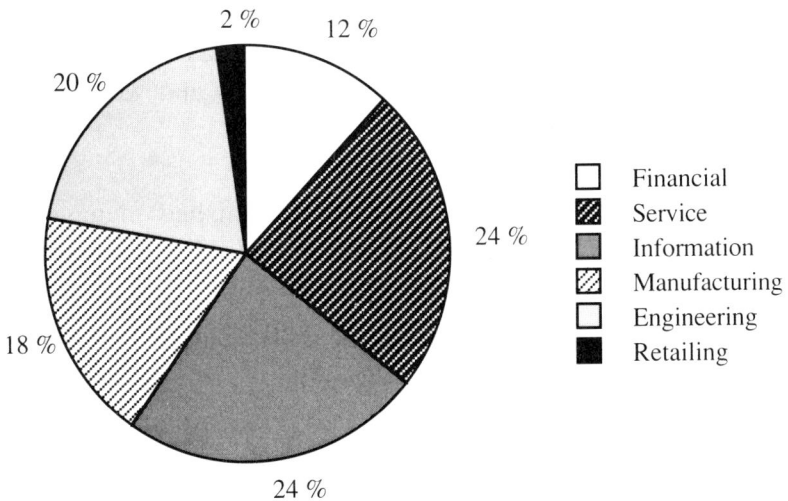

Figure 2 Response according to industrial sector.

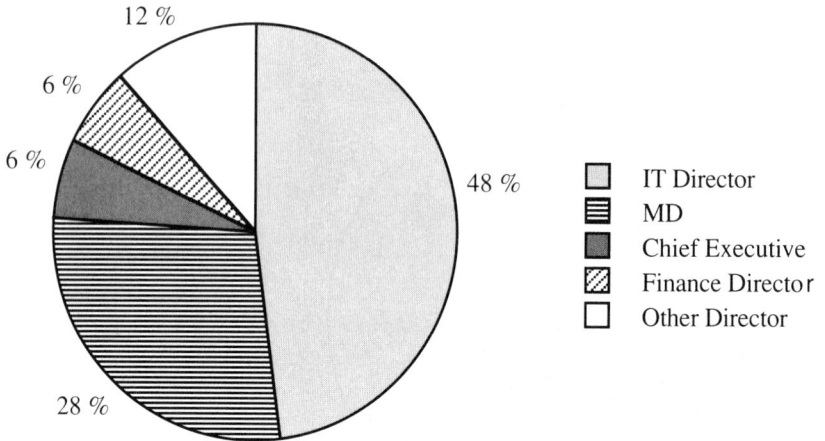

	IT Director
	MD
	Chief Executive
	Finance Director
	Other Director

Figure 3 Response according to managerial postition.

Analysing the overall response obtained, the following trends can be observed:

*   As was noted in previous research, UK companies are very much concerned about the effective use of IT and are willing to discuss and share the relative strengths and weaknesses of their own IT involvement.

*   Time and familiarity have not diminished management's concern for the eventual outcome of their IT investments.

*   While larger companies undoubtedly have greater resources and can allocate larger amounts of money to IT, some problems continue to exist, common to all companies regardless of their size, industrial sector, or the size of their IT budget.

*   The level of the position of the people with responsibility for

IT investments shows that the management of IT is assuming an increasingly important role in the majority of companies, irrespective of market sector.

- Appointing an IT executive within companies is becoming an increasingly common practice and is providing the focal point for the development of an IT infrastructure. How successfully this becomes integrated within the company business structure is still a major cause for concern.

Whereas Phase One concentrated on finding statistical correlations between IT investment practice and market success, Phase Two has been directed towards gaining a more in-depth view of the factors that influence positively and negatively the control of IT investments.

APPENDIX B

ASSESSING ORGANISATIONAL PERFORMANCE

Studies on the effectiveness of corporate IT investment strategies often aim to establish an independent criteria of organisational performance (OP) against which different IT investment strategies can then be measured. This often entails classifying companies into leaders/laggers or overachievers/underachievers and to search for statistical correlations between each group and each strategy investigated.

However, researchers report that the process of assessing the true health of a company or of an individual business unit is fraught with difficulties:

- Detailed accounting procedures of companies are often found to be too varied to allow a straightforward reliable comparison of OP. The problem of obtaining a homogeneous set of performance data across industries and across different sized companies has been well documented. For instance, Glueck and Willis, 1979, provide an analysis of conflicting standards within accounting practices and San Miguel, 1977, point out, as an example, reliability problems with Compustat data. The problem is particularly salient when comparing small firms to business units in multi-industry companies as it has been found that while performance data gathered from very small firms are often distorted due to rapid company changes, performance data gathered from business units in multi-industry companies are often inextricably interwoven with corporate-wide data.

- Intra-industry and inter-industry variations make it difficult to compare the performance of companies across industry sectors. The problem is well documented. For instance, a study conducted by Beard and Dess in 1981 shows that the influence of overall sector performance is a significant predictor of company performance.

- True OP is a complex and multidimensional phenomenon which is dependent on past performance, current efforts and long-term strategic plans. To assess OP therefore defies a performance analysis based exclusively on accounting practices. Again, the problem is well documented, see eg. Ford and Schellenberg's 1982 analysis on the inherent limitations of an exclusively economic framework to conceptualise OP.

To overcome these difficulties, researchers will have to develop more sophisticated methods of analysis when classifying companies and business units into leaders and laggers, or suffer the consequence that, when contrasting the OP of a company to particular IT investment strategy, the results will be confused.

A methodology to assess the organisational performance of companies currently under development at the Kobler Unit addresses each of these areas:

- To minimise the problems of varying accounting procedures, the Unit shifts the emphasis from the collection of static data to calculating more reliable dynamic developments of company performance. To do so, the growth ratios of after tax return on total assets, turnover, total operating costs and total sales are established by collecting data for two points in time, last year and two years before that.

- To minimise the effects of intra-industry and inter-industry variations, the calculated growth ratios are then adjusted with respect to the growth ratios of the market sectors within which a company competes.

- To broaden the assessment of OP beyond a purely accountancy framework, a number of additional factors are collected. These include a review of a company's strategic plans for a medium and longer-term horizon and the use of information services such as EXTEL and McCarthy for the purpose of gauging how the firm is perceived by independent market analysts. Furthermore, it is attempted to establish the level of customer complaints, critical staff turnover and general staff morale.

It is realised that research into assessing organisational performance is still in its infancy and that the above suggestions are not conclusive. However, if correlations must be drawn between the 'health' of a company and its strategy to deal with IT investments, and if significant correlations found doing so are taken as pointers prescribing good practice, researchers into the effectiveness of IT investments must make a stronger effort to come to grips with the subject. We hope that the above suggestions will contribute to that effort.

APPENDIX C

ASSESSING IT COSTS

The first step towards evaluating a new IT initiative is to formulate an IT procurement list with a detailed costing structure. The current research has found that many companies do not appreciate the true costs of installing IT and as a result underestimate total spend. In order to facilitate the costing process, and to thereby gain a more reliable evaluation of IT initiatives and a more effective control of a company's IT investments, the Kobler Unit has drawn up a check-list of the most common cost elements that are often left unspecified when proposing - and evaluating - further IT investments:

1. Hardware costs

Hardware costs are not just limited to buying pure processing power, be it mainframes, minis or PCs. Further expenditure is always needed for display units, primary and secondary data storage, printers or plotters and accessories.

2. Software costs

The cheapest solution by far is to introduce 'off the shelf' packages if they are adequate for the particular task at hand. However, this may still entail considerable costs to actually install the package, to build bridges to other applications, and to fine-tune the program to a particular user's precise needs.

The second cheapest solution is to invest in an application generator. Application generators need some limited programming skills to implement specific layouts and screens. If the package and the associated language is well known to the user, the programming and implementation can be done in a few days. If the generator is not known, the work can take up to several months as the new programming environment has first to be absorbed. In this case one should seriously consider employing an outside consultant as implementation costs and time can be fixed.

Custom-made software is the most expensive solution and varies in cost considerably, depending on the use of either low or high level languages. Whereas applications written in low level languages tend to be more time consuming and cost more initially, software in high level languages is more quickly developed but the final implementation might not perform as efficiently as expected, particularly when large amounts of data are involved. To subsequently introduce special routines simply to speed things up, will be an additional cost.

3. Installation costs

Installation efforts vary considerably, depending on the application and the hard/software environment in use. While, e.g. the installation of a spreadsheet package or a word processor on a PC is quite straightforward, the installation of document-sharing facilities over a UNIX network is a time-consuming process costing several man-weeks, possibly incurring further costs for expert advice.

If a paper-based activity is to be computerised, the costs of inputting current records needs to be considered.

4. Environmental costs

IT installations often necessitate changes in the physical environment. These might include underfloor wiring, extensive cabling, air conditioning, new lighting or additional furniture.

5. Running costs

Even though the electrical power consumption of an individual PC is very low, the combined power consumption of all the machines, including printers, plotters and disk drives is considerable - particularly as the equipment is often left operating continuously. New and more sophisticated machines consume more electrical power - e.g. colour screens use up to three times as much power as black and white screens, laser printers up to five times as much as dot matrix printers.

If external databases are to be accessed, include access fees, computer charge times and telephone bills.

6. Maintenance costs

Service and maintenance support has to be planned for. It is advisable to take out a comprehensive maintenance contract with a supplier as equipment breakdown can prove very expensive in terms of disrupting the business.

7. Security costs

The costs of ensuring that information held is not lost or interfered with requires additional investments in security procedures for holding and circulating classified information and for providing regular back-ups for all information and transactions. All systems need to be adequately supported by duplicates being maintained, preferably at off-site locations, in case of catastrophic loss that may well obliterate entire business areas.

8. Networking costs

Local and Wide Area Networks to share both information and hardware devices like printers or data storage systems often need the additional expenditure of dedicated workstations.

9. Training costs

Training costs are often more extensive than originally envisaged. While in-house training courses demand considerable resources for generating adequate training packages, outside training courses are expensive. Moreover, training is not a one-off activity and the necessity of planning update courses will become evident as users become more familiar with IT installations and as companies aim to ensure optimal use of sophisticated equipment.

10. Wider organisational costs

To identify and quantify the wider organisational costs is difficult. However, an effort has to be made to judge the following potential costs:

- Incompatibility costs: the implications of not buying compatible equipment need thorough and serious considerations.

- New salary structures: training people to use - and possibly program - sophisticated computer equipment will result in upgrading their jobs and salaries.

- Transitional costs: the introduction of new systems often incurs costs because of temporary job interruptions as prospective users will not be able to maintain their normal degree of productivity while learning how to use new equipment.

- Management costs: considerable management time may be needed to be spent on meetings, courses, training, security reviews, audit verification, counselling and explaining policies.

BIBLIOGRAPHY

Aleksander Igor, 'Information Technology and the Management of Change', *Journal of Information Technology*, February 1986, Volume 1 Number 1

Aleksander Igor, *'Business Computing and Communications'*, May 1987

Amdahl Research Report, 'Clues to Success: Information Technology, Strategies for Tomorrow', April 1988

Beard, D. and Dess, G., 'Corporate-level strategy, business-level strategy and firm performance', *Academy of Management Journal*, December 1981

Booz, Allen & Hamilton, 'CEO Study', March 1989

Boynton A.C. & Zmud R.W., 'An Assessment of Critical Success Factors', MIT, *Sloan Management Review*, Summer 1984

BIM Survey, 'Managers and IT Competence', BIM, 1988

BIM Report, The Responsive Organisation, People Management: The Challenge of the 1990's', BIM, 1989

CBI, 'Maintaining the Momentum of the Economic Recovery', *Economic Priorities for 1988*, CBI, 1988

Concensus Executive Briefing 1989 Series, Institute of Directors, 1989

Department of Trade and Industry 'Information Technology: Government's Response to the First Report of the House of Commons Trade and Industry Committee: 1988-89 Session', HMSO, 1989

Earl, M., 'Strategic Information Systems Planning in UK companies: Early Results of a Field Study', Working Paper, Oxford Institute of Information Management, Templeton College, Oxford, 1990

Earl, M., 'An Exploration into the Leadership and Management of the Information Systems Function', Working Paper, Oxford Institute of Information Management, Templeton College, Oxford, 1988

Earl M., 'Information Systems Strategy Formulation', in *Critical Issues in Information Technology Systems Research*, edited by R J Boland and R Hirschheim,Wiley & Sons, 1987

Ford, J.D. and Schellenberg, D.A., 'Conceptual issues of linkage in the assessment of organizational performance', *Academy of Management Review*, January 1982

Gibson C.F. & Jackson B.B., *The Information Imperative: Managing the Impact of Information Technology on Businesses and People, The Approach of the Index Group*, Lexington, 1987

Glueck, W.G. and Willis, R., 'Documentary sources and strategic management research', *Academy of Management Review*, January 1979

Hirschheim R.A., *Office Automation: A Social and Organizational Perspective*, John Wiley & Sons, 1985

Hirschheim R.A. & Smithson S., 'A Critical Evaluation of Information Systems Evaluation', Working Paper, Oxford Institute of Information Management, Templeton College, Oxford, 1986

Hochstrasser, B. & Griffiths, C., 'Does Information Technology Slow You Down', Kobler Unit, 1987

Hochstrasser, B., 'Assessing the Effectiveness of IT: Groundwork for a Knowledgebase', Imperial College, 1987

Hofer, C. and Schendel, D, *Strategy Formulation: Analytical Concepts*, West, St. Paul, 1978

IBM, 'Information Systems Planning Guide', IBM Corporation, 1981

Institute of Administrative Management & Confederation of British Industries, 'Corporate Organisation and Overhead Effectiveness Survey', A.T.Kearney, 1987

Ives, B. & Learmonth, G.P., 'The Information System as a Competitive Weapon', in Somogyi & Galliers, Abacus

Press, 1987

Kearney, A.T., 'Corporate Organisation and Overhead Effectiveness Survey', A.T. Kearney, 1987

Keen, P.G.W., *Competing in Time, Using Telecommunications for Competitive Advantage*, Ballinger, 1986

Laudon, K.C. & Turner, J., ed. *Information Technology and Management Strategy,* Prentice Hall, 1989

McFarland, F.W. and McKenney, J.L., *Corporate Information Systems Management*, Irwin, 1983

Management Programme Conference Papers,'IT and Organisational Change: Making IT Happen', 1989

OASiS, 'A Report on The Management of Marketing Information', OASiS, 1989

OECD, 'New Technology in the 1990s: A Socio-economic Strategy', OECD, 1988

PA Consulting Group, 'Top Management Information Systems in Whitehall', PA Consulting Group, 1989

Peat Marwick, 'IT Survey among CEOs', Peat Marwick, 1989

Peters, G.,'Evaluating Your Computer Investment Strategy', *Journal of Information Technology,* September 1988, Volume 3 Number 3

Porter, M.E., Competitive Strategys, Free Press, 1980

Price Waterhouse, 'Information Technology Review 1987/88', P.W., 1987

Price Waterhouse, 'Information Technology Review 1988/89', P.W., 1988

Price Waterhouse, 'Information Technology Review 1989/90', P.W., 1989

Rockart, J.F., 'Chief executives define their own data needs', *Harvard Business Review*, 1979, March/April: 81-93

Somogyi, E.K. & Galliers, R.D., ed. *Towards Strategic Information Systems*, Abacus Press, 1987

Strassmann, P.A., *Information Payoff*, Macmillan, 1985

Stuart, James, 'Strategy: The Pay-off Principle', *Business Computing and Communications*, February 1988

The Training Agency, *Training in Britain*, HMSO, 1989

Tomlin, R., 'Clues to Success: Information Technology, Strategies for Tomorrow', Research Report, April 1988

Trade and Industry Committee First Report Information Technology Volume 1 Report, HMSO, 1988

Wilson, T., 'Information System Strategies in UK Companies', University of Sheffield/Arthur Andersen Study, 1988

INDEX